Feng-Shui for Beginners

Physical and Magical Place Design

Contact: www.HarryEilenstein.de
Harry.Eilenstein@web.de
Harry Eilenstein at youtube

Production and publishing house: BoD – Books on Demand, Norderstedt

ISBN: 9783754301623

Feng Shui

=

Wind and Water

Table of Contents

I Life Force

"Feng Shui" is a Chinese term meaning "wind and water" – these are the two things that move most obviously in nature.

The subject of Feng Shui is the movements of the life force in external things. Consequently, Feng Shui is something like the acupuncture lore of nature or the chakra lore of landscape. The two terms "water" and "air" indicate the movements and flow of the elements, which has been associated with the life force. The life force (Chinese: "Chi") is sometimes personified in this context as water spirits and air spirits.

There is also an older term for Feng Shui, which is "Kanyu" and is a development of the older "hamjyu", which means "looking at the mountain and the land": Kanyu describes the activity in Feng Shui.

There are two sides to Feng Shui: One side is concerned with recognizing the life force and its conditions, and the other side is concerned with influencing the life force. In medicine this corresponds to diagnosis and therapy.

The second side of Feng Shui, i.e. directing the life force, has again two parts: On the one hand directing the life force with the help of physical changes and with the help of objects and on the other hand with the help of direct influence on the life force, i.e. by magic (will and imagination).

Feng Shui was created in a traditional way, i.e. by observation and experience – it is not an analytical system described by a logical system like mathematics. This means for the one who wants to know something about Feng Shui that he has to try out one or the other, because Feng Shui cannot be recognized as right or wrong by abstractly looking at the experiences gathered in Feng Shui – and also not by judging the inner logic of a system (which does not exist in this form in Feng Shui).

Feng Shui as a pure collection of experiences can of course be complemented by experiences in other areas. These other areas include power places, leylines, family constellations, astrology and crop circles. They are included in this introduction to Feng Shui.

The term "geomancy" actually means "earth divination" and is used to refer to an oracle in which signs were carved into the ground. Today it is largely used synonymously with Chinese "Feng Shui".

II The Analysis

The first step in Feng Shui is to be able to recognize the forms in a place and their effects, and on this basis then to be able to describe the quality of this place accurately. In addition to these intellectual, that is, analytical method, there are also some direct ways of recognizing the state of the life force at a certain place.

II 1. Observations in nature

The landscape and its elements, as well as the simple forms and conspicuous places, are the foundation of the observations in Feng Shui.

II 1. a) The quality of places

First of all, the general qualities of the elements of the landscape are considered in Feng Shui: Mountains, volcanoes, hills, gorges, valleys, seas, lakes, springs, rivers, shores, coasts, marshes, swamps, floodplains, forests, deserts, wastelands, pastures, fields, gardens, houses, cities, roads, bridges, railroads, etc.

The character of these elements of the landscape can essentially be discerned simply by looking at the element in question.

When looking at a specific place, knowing the qualities of these elements makes it easier to recognize the quality and life force dynamics in that place.

Mountain: concentration of the life force, connection upwards, independence, cohesion of the life force inside, flow of the life force on the surface, contact with the great movements of the life force in the wind, slowing down (on the slope), meeting of earth and air, masculine

Volcano: fire, rise of life force, kundalini, concentration, upheaval, transformation, great power, encounter of earth and fire

Mountain range: barrier, separation, inner tensions, high energy level, connection to the top, place of the sources of the great rivers

Gorge: separation, depth, gathering, breakthrough through a mountain range, the hidden becomes visible, access, entrance, passage, encounter with the earth

Cave: interior, hidden, protection, security, darkness, encounter with the earth, feminine

Valley: collection, relaxation, slowing down, rest, contemplation

Sea: depth, vastness, mystery, separation, great power

Lakes: collection, contemplation, tranquility, looking into the depths, meditation, dream journey

Source: origin, access to the underworld, life-giver

River: movement, flow, separation, revitalization

Shore: border, pause, separation, meeting of earth and water

Cut bank (outer curve of a river bend, against which the flowing water flows and erodes the bank there): release of life force to the bank, attack.

Slip-off lope (inner curve of a river bend, from which the water flows away and deposits sand and gravel there): deposition, absorption of vital force, relaxation.

Deposition (e.g. where a mountain stream enters a valley and deposits in a semi-circle the sand and gravel washed along with it): the bud shape shows that something has been brought there from one area (mountain) to another area (valley level) – enrichment, nourishment, increase

Mouth (tributary into main river): enlargement, union, increased concentration

Delta (river mouth into the sea): surrender, dissolution, slowing down, transformation

Coast: border, separation, meeting of earth and water, connection to wind

Fjord: separation, gathering, hollowing, splitting

Headland: insecure place, connection to the sea, view into the sea, open, connection to the wind

Island: separation, independence, strong connection to the water or the sea

Swamp (soggy earth, morass): connection of earth and water, danger, hidden, dissolution

Marsh (overgrown lake): connection of earth and water, danger, hidden, dissolution, depth, unknown, gate to the otherworld

Floodplain: borderland, meeting of earth and water, fertility, alluvium, passivity

Oxbow lake (of a river): stagnation, silence, flourishing, hidden, sedimentation

Forest: liveliness, the unknown, wilderness, the unformed

Forest edge: encounter between nature and culture, between open and hidden, between light and dark, between vastness and narrowness, therefore a great dynamism and diversity

Glade: openness, gathering, free space, attention

Steppe: little vitality, encounter of earth and wind, wilderness

Heath: medium life force, wilderness

Desert: little life force, wilderness

Wasteland: little life force, abandoned place, wildness

Minerals: imprinting of the basic radiation of a place => imprinting of the structures that preferentially form in a place (e.g. volcanic rock = much power; alluvial rock = relaxation; limestone rock = constructive structure formation)

Plants: imprinting of the secondary radiation of a place (plants need minerals and water to live) => imprinting of the postures that form preferentially at a place

Animals: imprinting of the tertiary radiation of a place (animals need plants to live) => imprinting of the dynamics which are preferably formed at a place

Pasture: low life force, connection with animals, little formed

Fields: increased vitality, connection with plants, more strongly designed

Gardens: much vitality, connection with plants, strongly designed

House: protection, shell, living space, people, very strongly designed

City: little life force, very strongly shaped

City wall: protection, separation

Temple or Church: place of contemplation, connection upwards, source of life force and community identity

Shop or Market: exchange, meeting, distribution of vitality, meeting point

Station: departure, change, movement

Castle: protection, defense, demarcation, dominance, gathering of life force from the surrounding space

Tower: protection, farsightedness, superiority, sometimes a connection to the top

Palace: Ruling place, charisma, steering, dominance

Skyscraper: dominance, imprint

Barracks: power, domination, command

Cemetery: rest, end, reflection, transformation

Capital: center, steering, dominance, gathering of life force

Street: movement, connection of cities, straight movement, separation in nature

Crossroads: center, structuring, choice, rigidity

Distributing circle: center, structuring, possibility of choice, circular movement

Fork in the road: possibility of choice, pressure on what is in the fork in the road

Bridge: Connection, new flow possibility for the life force

Railroad line: movement, connection of cities, separation in nature

Power lines: movement, hard-imprinted life force, main artery of civilization, separation in nature

II 1. b) The qualities of simple forms

There is a whole series of simple shapes such as straight lines, arcs, corners, breaks, points, circles, etc., which have the same qualities in all places where they appear.

Straight line: The straight line accelerates and focuses the life force – it corresponds to a laser beam. It makes the life force become hard and hurtful.
Therefore, longer straight lines are avoided as much as possible in Feng Shui.

10

Arc: It makes the life force vibrate and become soft. Arcs give rhythm to the life force.

Therefore, in Feng Shui, all larger forms are curved, or all longer straight forms, such as roof edges, are ended with an arc.

Corner: Here two straight lines or surfaces (which are therefore "hard") meet each other – usually at right angles. Consequently, corners are a particularly "hard" place.

Therefore corners are often rounded or columns are placed at them or a tree is planted in front of them to intercept the hard life force at these corners, to disperse it or to let it become softer and more organic.

Tip: It is the end of one or more straight surfaces that end at a point. The hard life force of the straight surfaces does not collide here with the hard life force of the other side, as it does at a corner, but it is concentrated and sent out at the tip.

Therefore, such points are avoided as much as possible in Feng Shui, since it is believed that the life force ray emanating from such a point has an injurious effect. Such a ray is similar to one person pointing his finger at another all the time – which is quite unpleasant …

Pyramid: It occurs mainly as a tomb and corresponds to the mountain: a far visible connection upwards to the ancestors and the gods …

Fractures: They interrupt the flow, they are therefore like wounds or blockages. They are avoided as much as possible in Feng Shui.

Circles: They form a closed system – they enclose, protect, exclude, isolate, concentrate, create an interior space …

Circles can therefore be used in a variety of ways in Feng Shui, but this is limited to smaller shapes, since a circle tends to generate hard, i.e. tightly focused life force, due to its uniform shape, like the straight line.

Horseshoe: In such a shape, something is gathered, that comes from the edges, but then allowed to flow back out through the opening in a soft form. Valleys can have this form – in them the waters of several streams gather, which then leave the valley as a small river. Such valleys contain a lot of soft life force, especially in their center.

This is a very popular shape in Feng Shui, as it allows for soft, relaxed concentration. The center of such a valley has been a popular place for temples and tombs in China.

Open forms: Open forms collect and release what has been collected in a more concentrated form.

Cosed forms: Closed forms collect, but delimit and isolate.

11

Pain: On a level, all points are largely equal.

Rise: Towards the top, the energy level increases and so does the concentration and, in some cases, the hardness or concentratedness of the life force.

Descent: Towards the bottom, the energy level and thus also the concentration and in some cases also the hardness or concentratedness of the life force decreases.

II 1. c)   The qualities of special places

Finally, there are some places that have a special quality – some of them have already been discussed.

Places of power: These are places with significantly increased life force, such as some valleys and mountains, like volcanoes, temples, places of worship, stone circles, capitals, government buildings, castles, and the like. These points on the earth correspond to the chakras and the acupuncture-points in humans.

Leylines: This term refers to the lines along which life force flows from one place to another. They correspond to the acupuncture meridians in humans, on which the acupuncture points are located. In China, a leyline would be called a dragon path, the path along which much life force flows.

Crop circles: There are some places where crop circles occur almost every year and where the largest and most impressive crop circles are also found such as Alton Barnes' field near the White Horse in Wiltshire in southern England. These are special, "creative" places of power.

Haunted houses: One can also count haunted houses among the power places, although the haunting is a secondary and rather disturbing force at this place …

II 1. d)   The qualities in a house

There are also different places in a house, which have approximately the same character in each house. Only the most important and common of them are enumerated below:

Entrance: border, gate, skin, protection

Corridor: distributor, movement

Living room: recreation center, meeting, conviviality

Bay window: extension, accentuation, emphasis, specialness, view

Bedroom: relaxation, rest

Kitchen: processing center, center of vitality

Bathroom: relaxation, purification

Loo: letting go, cleansing

Storeroom: supplies, life force

Basement: supplies, stored things, hidden things, machines (heating, etc.)

Boiler room: warmth, root chakra, life force production

Attic: crown chakra, head

Staircase: life force channel (sushumna, ida and pingala, acupuncture meridians)

Floors: Chakras
- **Basement** = root chakra
- **Ground floor** (kitchen) = hara, solar plexus
- **2nd floor** (living room) = heart chakra
- **3rd floor** (meeting rooms) = throat chakra, third eye
- **Attic rooms** = crown chakra

Roof: protection

Sauna: relaxation, letting go

II 2.   Grasping the place with the help of the Ba Gua

The qualities of the different parts of a single place can be grasped with the help of the Ba Gua. The Ba Gua is a reliable grid of nine areas, in which each of the nine areas has a specific meaning.

This grid exists not only in China, but also in India, where it has been named after the primordial giant Purusha as "Vashtu Purusha".

II 2. a)   The nine areas of the grid

The quality of the nine surfaces is obtained in a simple way by combining the properties of the vertical columns with the properties of the three horizontal rows. These properties are:

- upper row:	high energy level
- middle row:	medium energy level
- lower row:	low energy level
- left column:	Past
- middle column:	Present
- right column:	Future

The qualities of the three lines result from the fact that one must use energy to lift something up.

The qualities of the three columns result from the fact that on the northern hemisphere, on which China and also by far the largest part of the inhabited continents are located, one sees the sun, the moon and the stars always moving from left to right.

Thus the nine qualities result that are shown in the following overview. The terms written normally are derived from the quality of the rows and columns; the terms written in *italics* are derived from traditional Feng Shui.

The qualities of the nine fields		
much energy + past = sponsor, helper *abundance, prosperity*	much energy + present = coronation, fame *fame, prestige*	much energy + future = goal, ideal *relationships, love*
medium energy + past = family of origin *parents, support*	middle energy + present = center, middle, theme *ego, power, health*	middle energy + future = own family *children, creativity*
little energy + past = starting point, learning *knowledge, learning*	little energy + present = foundation, support *profession, savings*	little energy + future = rest, failure *travel, helper*

II 2. b)   The grid of Ba Gua at a place

This grid is placed over the place whose qualities one wants to grasp. The place is surrounded with a rectangle in such a way that as little area of the place under consideration as possible is not covered and also as little area as possible that does not belong to the place is covered.

In the Ba-Gua, "down" is always where the main access to the place is.

In the diagram, the place is a rectangle with curved sides; the access path to it is the vertical line.

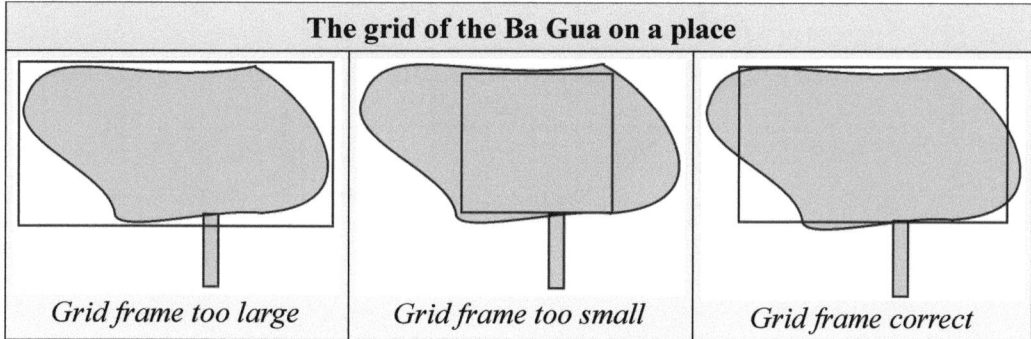

The grid of the Ba Gua on a place		
Grid frame too large	*Grid frame too small*	*Grid frame correct*

Next, the grid is divided into nine equal areas. There are sometimes (as in this example) areas that are not in the grid, as well as outer areas that are in the grid. Since rectangular areas such as plots of land or house layouts are very often considered, these surplus or missing areas occur only occasionally.

In the previous example the correctly placed grid would look like this:

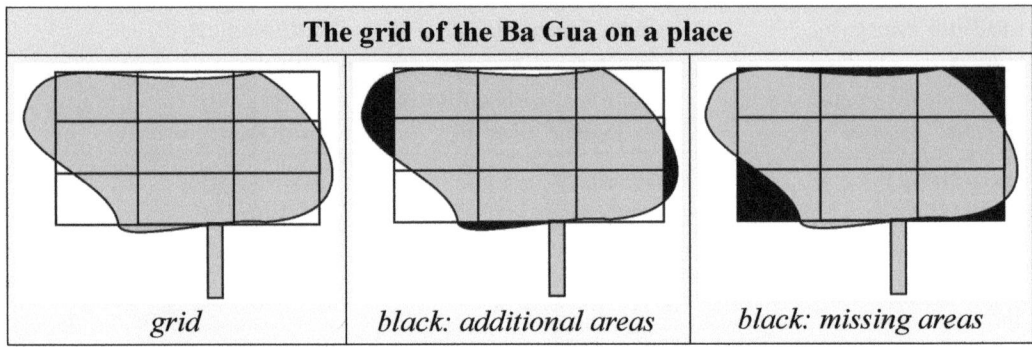

The grid of the Ba Gua on a place

| grid | black: additional areas | black: missing areas |

II 2. c) Abundance and lack in the grid

If we now examine the example place shown above, we find that some of these nine areas have been strengthened by additional areas and others have been weakened by missing areas:

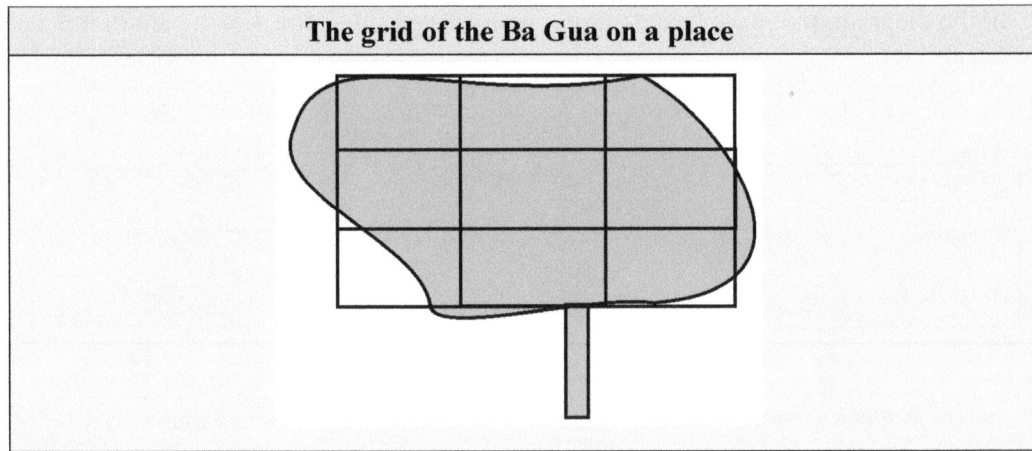

The grid of the Ba Gua on a place

The area on the upper left of this site, for example, is strengthened by a bulge. This indicates that the owner of this plot is supported by others with money and the like.

The additional area on the left in the center indicates that the person in question is also supported by his parents in relation to his property.

The more than half missing area on the lower left indicates that the person has done little to own this property.

The small missing area at the top center indicates that the subject gains only very little (of any) esteem by posseing this place.

The two grid areas at the bottom right and the center right both have a missing area and a complementary area – this adds a bit of unrest to them. For the grid area on the bottom right, this means that resting on the property is sometimes difficult, and for the grid area on the center right, this means that there may be difficulties with children and with creativity.

The missing area on the upper right indicates that one may not achieve the goals one had in mind with this plot and that there may be relationship problems.

II 2. d) Objects in the grid

If it is a plot of land, you can now look to see where there are trees, where there is a pond, where there is a rock, where there is a hollow, where there is a hill, etc..

A hill in the upper right area would strengthen the achievement of the goals, and a hollow in that location would weaken it even further.

A pond in the middle area would make this plot a place of introspection.

Several trees in the upper middle area would enhance prestige, etc.

II 2. e) Paintings in the grid of Ba Gua

This method of viewing with the help of the Ba Gua may also be applied to paintings – such as the painting "Starry Night" by Vincent van Gogh.

Vincent van Gogh: Sternennacht

At the top right (aims) is the moon as the most striking element in the painting – it was the motivation for painting. Is this motivation a (hidden) dream?

Below is a city on the low level – van Gogh wanted to go beyond this level.

On the left, a thuja or something similar towers darkly – the striving for a higher level of energy, which has not led to much in the past, as it remains dark. Thus, the moon is the symbol of reaching a goal that has not been reached in the past. The dark tree cuts of the past from the present and the future – does this indicate a loss? And does the moon symbolise the longing for this lost thing? Maybe a loved person van Gogh has lost?

Mountains rise from the lower left to the center right – a dark line of mountains below, a lighter line of mountains above. The line rising upwards to the right is the movement of hope for better times (an energy level rising toward the future). The light above the dark has the same optimistic meaning.

From the upper left, a vortex enters the center, but then runs out to the center right. This is hope for help from outside – perhaps also hope for a woman's approval of a relationship, since the line ends in the center right, where the self-founded family is located. There, on the far right in the center, the contrast of dark and light is also strongest – the essence of the drama of the feelings underlying this picture.

II 2. f) Drawings in the grid of the Ba Gua

In order to be able to recognize that the Ba Gua really works, one should try it out several times. You can also let someone draw a few lines on a sheet of paper – and then with the help of the Ba Gua you can describe very precisely the momentary mood of the this person.

The grid of the nine fields should only be added after the drawing has been made by drawing additional lines or by folding the paper used four times (two times horizontal, two times vertical). If you draw the grid before, it would distract the other person.

Example 1

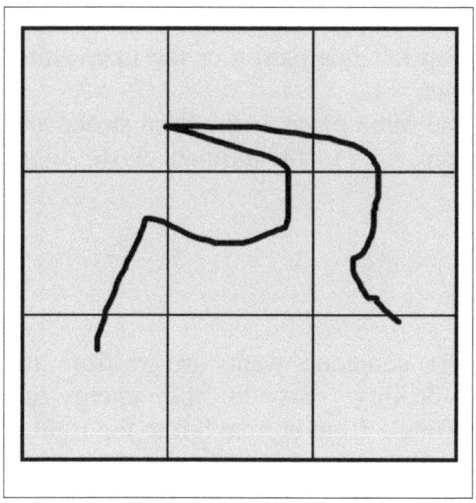

In the drawing on the left, the drawer started the line on the lower left (one should observe the person drawing and remember the direction and order of the strokes).

The impulse started at a low level in the past (bottom left) – the person probably wants to change an unpleasant situation.

He rises with momentum to the middle level, but then bends sharply to the lower right: His momentum, his effort does not last long.

From the middle field, i.e. out of himself, he turns to the upper left (high energy in the past): he hopes for help from outside from a supporter – he wants something, but he cannot achieve it out of his own strength.

After this request for help, he strives upwards to the right towards his ideal, but then trundles downwards (low energy) on the future side (right): his impulse to improve his situation with external help has failed …

Example 2

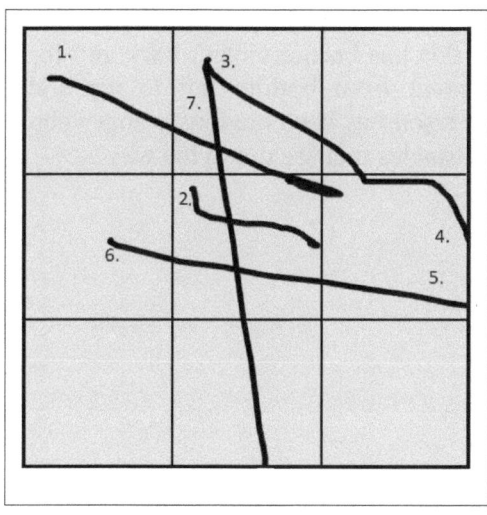

The strokes have been drawn almost furiously – between point 4. and 5. the line has even over been drawn over the edge and also the line that starts at point 7. has been drawn over the sheet at the bottom.

The first line that has been drawn starts at point 1. One wants to get help from the field on the upper left and anchor it in itself in the middle – a hook has been painted there.

The second line that has been drawn starts at point 2. and repeats the movement of the first line with clearly less verve and exclusively in the central field, i.e. within the ego.

The next stroke begins at point 3. and is

like an angry repetition of the two previous strokes – but here, too, no more asking for help in the upper left field. The stroke crashes, goes angrily beyond the edge of the paper (4.) and then shoots back (from 5.) to the left to point 6.: a massive, angry, accusatory regression – the subject is convinced that he is entitled to something specific from the top left or middle left field. Top left is a patron or the like; center left is the family of origin – presumably the mother.

Finally, a fourth stroke (at point 7.) starts at the same place as the third stroke and shoots steeply down within the middle column (present, I) – the ultimate crash. Anger and depression …

Example 3

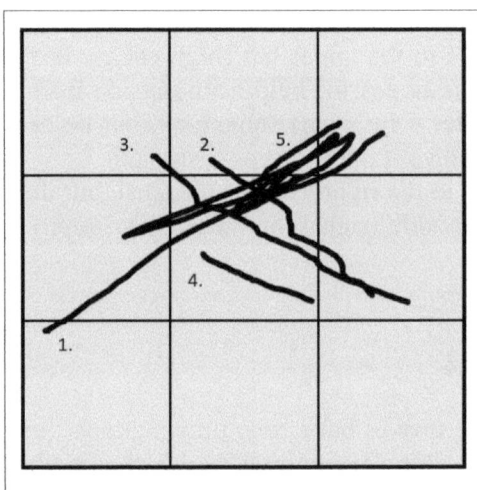

Here someone wants to go from the energy-lacking past to the energy-rich future (line 1 from bottom left to top right).

But there are obstacles: the three lines starting at point 2., 3. and 4: They lie across the desired ascent to the high energy level in the future (top right).

But the person does not let himself be intimidated: At point 5 he begins to draw five connected lines from the lower left to the upper right and back – he wants to assert himself and overcome the obstacles (crossing lines). From the drawing point of view, this has been a violent back and forth movement from bottom left to top right. This person has been obviously angry about the obstacles that are put in his way …

II 3. The surrounding space

The consideration of the place, whose quality one wants to understand, is now followed by the consideration of the surrounding space. There are several methods for this.

II 3. a) The Ba Gua in the surrounding space

The considered place is now the middle field of the Ba Gua – the Ba Gua itself extends over the entire surrounding space. "Below" is still the side of this place where the main access is located.

Now one has a look at what striking landscape features are found around this place. In the example on the left, there are five distinctive elements around the considered place.

The place under consideration is a plot of land (the dark gray field in the middle).

A mountain at the top left would, for example, strengthen the influence of donors and other benevolent persons and give them a great influence.

A ravine above the upper middle field would limit fame and prestige.

A bend in the river to the left of center, where the river first flows toward the site and then away from it, would provide the site with life force – which would presumably come to the site through the family of origin.

A pond in the lower right would greatly enhance the opportunities to relax on this property.

A power line is running straight toward the property from the right and turning at a right angle just before it would "bombard" the property with hard life force and thus weaken the right center field – i.e. that creativity is difficult at this place and that there my be harm to one's children.

II 3. b) The zodiac

If one knows the exact time when this property was acquired by its owner, one can calculate the horoscope for this property. First of all, this already tells quite a lot about this plot of land.

But you can also draw the horoscope around the plot of land – in such a way that the ascendant points exactly to the place on the eastern horizon where the sun rose on that day.

In this way the planets can be assigned to the different directions around the property. Thereby the zodiac forms as a ring around the property – and thus the assignment of the 12 zodiac qualities to the surrounding area of the property.

The center of the zodiac lies exactly in the center of the Ba Gua and also of the property which is considered here.

One can now look from the center of the plot to a place or object on the plot and then see in front of which zodiac sign it stands (sketch below left).

One can also look from the center to a planet in the chart (on the zodiac around the plot) and then see which of the eight outer areas it faces (sketch below right).

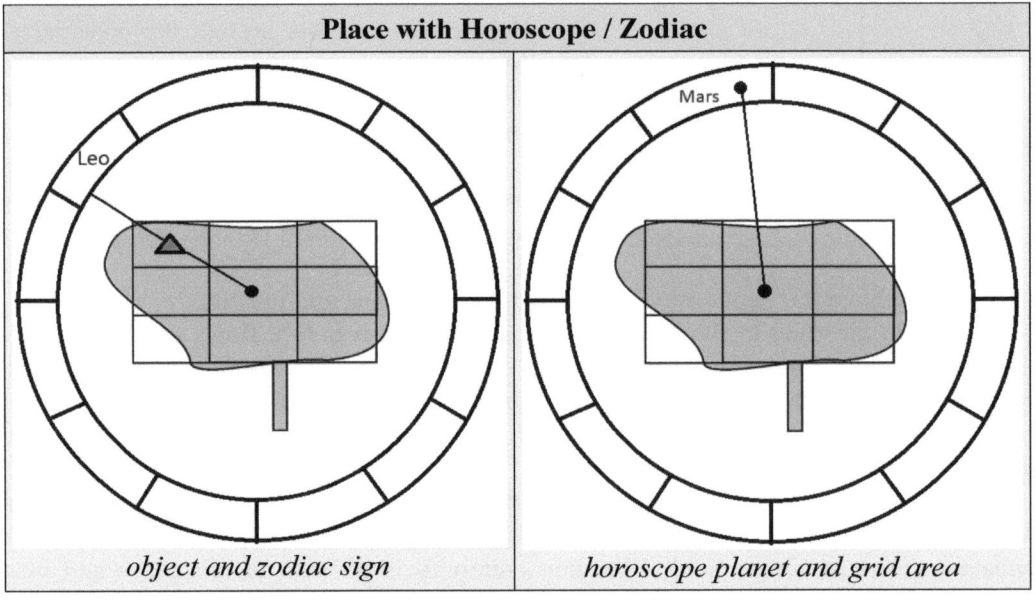

Place with Horoscope / Zodiac

| *object and zodiac sign* | *horoscope planet and grid area* |

As with all such methods, one should first test this procedure on a few examples and see how helpful one finds the results thus obtained before applying them in more important contexts.

II 3. c)   The Luopan

The "Luopan" or "Lo Pan" is a round map on which the qualities of the cardinal points are drawn in a very differentiated way. Up to 40 different groups of qualities are observed, which are then also drawn in 40 circles on this circular chart.

The center of the Luopan is a compass, with the help of which one puts the Luopan in the center of the considered place and aligns it to the north. Then, with the help of the different circular charts concentrically arranged around the compass, one can see the qualities of the different directions.

This procedure corresponds to the orientation to the zodiac in the previous chapter and also to the occidental assignment of the four elements to the four directions of the sky.

The Luopan is a collection of empirical values, which consequently cannot be recognized as right or wrong in an abstract way by logical conclusions – you have to try it out …

Probably it is easier (and therefore more reasonable) to use at first a simple system like the four elements or the zodiac or a simple variant of the Luopan.

Again, one should first try this method in a few places and look closely at its results before making decisions based on it for the evaluation and design of a place.

Personally, the Ba Gua seems to me to be more reliable than the general assignments to directions with the help of the four elements, the zodiac, the horoscope or the Luopan – but this is just my opinion.

II 4. Qualities

There are a number of qualities of the life force that are distinguished in Feng Shui.

The basic distinction is **"hard" and "soft"**, which also corresponds to "straight and curved" and "constant and rhythmic". "Soft, curved, rhythmic" is generally life-enhancing and "hard, straight, constant" is more life-hostile.

The best known contrast is certainly **Yin and Yang**. This model dates back to the early Neolithic period and can be found as a quality opposition already in the first temples of the people in Göbekli Tepe in northern Mesopotamia around 10,000 BC. Yin and Yang have originally been this world in the south of the tumulus and the otherworld in the north of the tumulus. From this, many other qualities have been derived:

Yang	Yin
this world	otherworld
body	soul
south side of the tomb	north side of the tomb
sun god	otherworld goddess
outside	inside
fire	Water
muspelheim (Teutons)	niflheim (Teutons)
sulphur (Alchemy)	mercury (Alchemy)
light	dark
white	black
day	night
summer	winter
fullness	emptiness
hot	cold
high	low
top	bottom
hard	soft
male	female
positive	negative
active	passive
moving	calm
dry	moist

etc.

However, the two terms "Yin" and "Yang" are rarely used today in their original sense of "this world" and "otherworld", but mainly in the sense of hard/male and soft/female.

The **three dynamics** can be found almost everywhere, but they are still little known. In astrology they appear in the zodiac as the three dynamics in which the four elements appear:

      1. cardinal, creating, impulse;
      2. fixed, shaping, boundary;
      3. mutable, linking, contact.

These three qualities are also found in the chakra system. Starting from the identity in the heart chakra, there are above and below

      - first the impulse (solar plexus + throat chakra → feelings),
      - then the forms (hara + third eye → mind)
      - and outside finally the contact (root chakra + crown chakra → perception).

These three dynamics can be found in any environment and are therefore also important in Feng Shui. For example, in a property

      - the house and the garden are formed by one's own impulse (1st area),
      - the fence formed the border (2nd area)
      - and the garden gate, the mailbox, the bell, the telephone connection etc. are the possibility of contact (3rd area).

In Europe and America the system of the **four elements** is widespread. Since it is already connected with the cardinal points and the seasons, it can be easily integrated into Feng Shui. As with all systems, one must try it out to see if its use is useful for oneself.

Air	*Fire*	*Water*	*Earth*
east	south	west	north
morning	noon	evening	night
spring	summer	autumn	winter
birth	life	death	beyond
hot/moist	hot/dry	cold/moist	cold/dry
truth	strength	love	thriving

Another system of four are the **four images** from the I Ching. They are the four possible combinations of yin and yang. These four images are:

Air/Sky	*Earth*	*Fire*	*Water*
is above	is below	rises	descends
old Yang	old Yin	young Yang	young Yin
Yang/Yang	Yin/Yin	Yin/Yang	Yang/Yin

In China the system of the **five elements** is of great importance. In this system, fire, water and air appear as in Europe, but the earth appears in two variants as metal and as wood. From the European point of view, wood is an organic synthesis of the four elements.

Another system of qualities are the **eight trigrams** from the I Ching, which result when the four images are combined one more time with Yin and Yang – there are altogether eight possibilities to combine Yin and Yang in a group of three.
These eight trigrams are: heaven, earth, fire, water (which correspond to the four images) as well as mountain, lake, wind and thunder.
Places can also be described in terms of these eight qualities.

From astrology, one can use the **ten planets** to describe the qualities of a place. If one is familiar with the qualities of the ten planets, this is a useful system.

The **twelve signs of the zodiac** also originate from astrology. However, they are not dynamics or processes like the planets, but styles. Therefore, they cannot be used in the same way as the planetary qualities. Viewing a place using the planets leads more to an action image, while using the zodiac signs leads more to a structure image.

The **sixty-four hexagrams** of the I Ching result from the combinations of the eight trigrams with each other (8·8=64). They represent processes rather than qualities, in contrast to the trigrams. This oracle may be used (just like Tarot cards) to get a general description of the main quality of a place.

- - -

One should first of all use for the description of a place the qualities and quality systems which one is already familiar with – in this way one will get the most precise description.

II 5. Systems

The same as for the different qualities applies to the systems one should use in the beginning – one should use the systems one is already familiar with. This can be the chakra system, the Kabbalah, astrology, the Tarot, the I Ching or any other system.

What matters first is to achieve a description of the place where one wants to do something that is as accurate as possible.

For this, in addition to a system, experience is, of course, necessary – without practice, you can't get a feel for it. In the end, it doesn't matter how you do it – the main thing is to start. Then perceptions, new questions, new ideas, other approaches, etc. will arise of their own accord and thereby further develop one's own ability to accurately describe the quality of a place.

The observation of the place should always be at the beginning – after all, one should have seen what one wants to recognize and understand. The descriptions of the landscape features and the house areas from chapter "II 1." can be used as aids.

Next, you can get creative. For example, one can draw and place a Tarot card at each distinctive point of the place and then look at what qualities the Tarot cards point to.

You can feel what qualities you perceive in the different places of the site and then draw them on a sketch of the site with the help of the planet symbols.

You can also light a match at each of the prominent places and see how it burns and conclude from this the quality of this place at the site to be examined.

The guiding principle should always be that this is about the site and not about the system – the system used is only a tool for knowing the qualities of the place under consideration.

II 6. Angles

One group of qualities that can be found in a place and that has not been described so far are the angles. There is a set of angles which have the same quality everywhere – no matter whether they are considered in geometry, in astrology (aspects) or in physics. Also the numerical ratios of the intervals in the music can be assigned to them. With the angles is also closely connected the "natural number symbolism".

So the angles are a basic symbolism, which is independent of the use of a certain system. They are as system-independent as e.g. the natural constants in physics (speed of light, gravitational constant, Planck constant, Feigenbaum constant etc.).

Consequently, when one encounters one of these angles at a site, one has a very reliable indication of the quality at the place where that angle occurs.

The seven angles that have a certain quality that can be reliably detected and described are:

0°: If the angle is 0°, everything remains as it is and there is no "kink". In astrology, this is the conjunction, which can be described as unification or identity preservation. In music, this is the prime interval (or the octave): you simply repeat the same note again. In physics this is the gravitation, which pulls all things to each other. This force is one-polar. As a number this is the "1".

This angle is normally not experienced as an angle, but as the absence of an angle.

180°: At this angle two things face each other because the circle has 360° and 180° is exactly half of it – this angle continues 1/2 of a circle. In astrology this ratio is called opposition. This angle has the quality of a complementary opposition. The best known example is probably the opposition of Yin and Yang, from which the endless movement and transformation results, which is described differentiated in the I Ching ("Book of Changes").

In music, this angle, which can also be described as "going half a circle further", can be found in the fifth, which has a frequency 1.5 times higher than the initial note, thus "going half a circle further".

In physics, this is the electromagnetic force: the two electric poles (+ and –) are opposites and so are the two magnetic poles (north and south). These two polarities cause a movement of the particles, which also have an electric and magnetic charge, respectively. This force is two-polar.

120°: Three angles of 120° form a circle (360°), so this angle continues 1/3 of a circle. In astrology this angle between two planets is called "trine". It is the connection of two related things to a pulsating unity. Three planets, each 120° apart, would form an equilateral triangle. These three planets would then all be in zodiac signs with the same element (e.g. fire), and these three zodiac signs would then be this element in its three dynamics (fire sign: Aries – Leo – Sagittarius). The three dynamics are therefore the quality of the 120° angle: coherence, organic form, development, unfolding, rhythm, etc.

The Kabbalistic Tree of Life is a differentiated representation of this dynamic of the 120° angle – just as the I Ching is a differentiated representation of the 180° angle. In physics, exactly the same basic structure as in the Kabbalistic tree of life is found in the mathematical model of the superstring theory: The Tree of Life consists of 11 areas and the mathematical model of the superstring theory has 11 dimensions. The qualities of these 11 components coincide in both.

Another physical example for the 120°-angle or for the "3" and the three dynamics are the three different sizes, in which the four elementary particles up-quark, down-quark, electron and neutrino, appear – from these four particles in their three sizes the whole world is built.

Finally, there is the third basic force in physics: the color force, which holds together the three quarks in the neutrons and protons. It is the strongest of all physical forces. This force is three-polar.

In music, the fourth has a frequency 1.33 times higher than the fundamental, i.e. it has 1/3 more vibrations per second than the fundamental. Thus it corresponds to the astrological trine. Finally, the same quality exists in crystal healing, where all minerals with triclinic crystallization form, based on 120° angles, have an organic joining, rhythmic effect.

90°: Four angles of 90° form a complete circle, so this angle continues 1/4 of a circle. The shape this creates is a square. Hence "square" is the name of the corresponding astrological aspect. Its quality is distinguishing, separating and demarcating – it is like a tent pole that separates two tarpaulins and thereby spans a space. This is why squares, i.e. right angles (90° angles) are found in large numbers in everything that is constructed and built up and rigid – such as the stones and walls and rooms of houses and also the house as a whole.

The 90° angle is also found between the four cardinal points, which together form a cross. They are also associated with the four elements. This number of elements is not a coincidence, as it is shown by the fact that there are exactly four basic elementary particles: up-quark, down-quark, electron and neutrino.

An important place in physics where the 90° angle is found is the relation between an electric wave and the corresponding magnetic wave (e.g. in a photon). These two waves form a cross, whose end points have the maximum distance from each other by the four 90° angles between them – which clearly shows the square quality of separation.

In music this angle is found at the interval "major third". This tone has a frequency 1.25 times higher than the fundamental, i.e. it goes 1/4 further.

Finally, the 90° angle can be found in crystal healing, where all the minerals with cubic crystallization form, that is, with 90° angles between the ions in the crystals, have an ordering, separating, delimiting, rigid effect.

60°: This angle joins equal elements into groups. This grouping is also the quality of the astrological sextile, which denotes the distance of 60°. This angle continues 1/4 of a circle. This angle shapes, for example, the angular distances between a large number of equal-sized balls in a bucket. On a small scale, this is found in the arrangement of protons and neutrons in an atomic nucleus. On a large scale, this is found in the orbit around a planet, where up to six moons can orbit one planet at the same time in the same orbit, each 60° apart.

The 60° angle is also the "optimization angle": spheres lie closest when they are at this angle to each other; spaces are most material-efficient when they are constructed as honeycombs, as bees do; surfaces are most material-efficient when they are constructed at 60° angles, like a snowflake; the shortest connection between the four corners of a square is achieved with the help of 60° angles (in this form: >–<); etc.

30°: The astrological aspect of the semi-sextile represents a further development. It is the advancement by 1/12 in a circle (360°:12=30°). This angle corresponds to the 12: the zodiac has 12 sections, the simplest super-string is a circle divided into 12 equal sections, and there are 12 elementary particles (four fundamental particles in three different sizes).

150°: The astrological aspect of the quincunx describes the constant re-orienting, re-ordering, re-spanning. It is difficult to prove in physics because of its dynamics – it is rather a process than a structure …

The angles of 30°, 90° and 150° are connected to the weak nuclear force, that always transforms the nucleus of an atom.

II 7. Natural Forms

It is worthwhile to take a closer look at the natural forms in the landscape to develop an eye for the character of a place. Almost all forces or processes on earth give rise to typical forms. This makes it possible to recognize on the basis of these forms the forces which have led to their development and which in many cases still are at work in them.

One can divide these forces into the four areas for the sake of clarity in fire, water, air and earth.

The two forces whose effect on the landscape is easiest to observe are water and air – that is why the art of recognizing these forces is also called "Feng Shui", i.e. "water (and) wind".

II 7. a) Fire

The hot lava in the earth gives rise to volcanoes, which appear either singly, in small groups, or in long rows. Their shapes range from pointed to flat. They are usually quite easy to recognize because they form individual, distinct peaks (or islands in the sea). They are places where there is easy access to the earth fire, that is, to the root chakra of the earth. Volcanoes are consequently suitable for charging the actions in this place with great power and making them very effective.

Lava fields have a rather watery form, as they flow from the volcano to the plain, where they gradually solidify.

Finally, there are lightning, forest fires, brush fires, and steppe fires, but these are all short-term phenomena.

The warming of the climate as a whole, which is, after all, also a "fire pheno-menon," can, on the other hand, have very profound and long-term effects.

A combination of fire and water is found in geysers, which are a jet of hot water and steam created when water in a cave in the earth is heated by the lava near it and then rises to the surface through a tube or fissure.

II 7. b) Water

The simplest and most familiar form of water is the wave – firstly as a wave on a stream, river, lake or sea, and secondly as the concentric circles caused, for example, by a stone thrown into water.

Rivers have the urge to flow straight ahead – their momentum carries them in the direction they are flowing. As a result, when they encounter an obstacle, they gradually erode and dissolve that obstacle. This happens on the cut bank, i.e. in the outer bend of the river – where soil and rocks are removed. On the other hand, soil is deposited on the slip-off slope, i.e. in the inner curve, and likewise in slow-flowing places, where islands can form as a result.

Waterfalls have a special dynamic, because the falling water in front of the waterfall digs a deep hole in the riverbed.

Lakes also have their own dynamics. They form where the landscape is lower in one place than all around – there the water from the creeks accumulates and cannot flow away. When enough water flows into this low area, the water level rises until the water can flow out of the valley at one point. Gradually, the stream or river leaving this valley-lake digs deeper and deeper into the land at its outflow point, causing the water level of the lake to drop again – the outflow gradually becomes deeper and takes the form of a narrow valley or gorge.

At the same time, the streams that flow into the valley carry soil into the lake that has formed there and gradually fill it up, ultimately creating a plain that is approximately at the level of the lake's water table.

Sometimes there are waterfalls in the stream or river that leaves the lake in this valley – for example, the Rhine Falls of Schaffhausen down the Rhine from Lake Constance. Waterfalls keep digging out the riverbed and thus gradually move upstream – the waterfall gradually causes the rocks over which it flows to fall and then wash away. When this waterfall finally reaches a lake, the outlet of this lake will be much deeper in a short time – then both the waterfall and a large part of the lake will disappear. The Rhine Falls will also reach Lake Constance one day, whereupon the Rhine Falls will then disappear and the water in Lake Constance will sink very much and become much smaller.

This process is already completed at the Upper Rhine Valley (from Basel to Frankfurt). This long valley has been filled up with alluvium by the rivers flowing into it, and the Rhine has already burrowed into the mountains to the north of the Upper Rhine Valley (from Bingen to Bonn) so deeply that there are no more waterfalls or appreciable gradients in these mountains.

In soil and soft rock, rivers create valleys, while in hard rock they create gorges.

In valleys and depressions, where little water flows in and little or no water flows out, swamps and bogs often form. If there are larger creeks or little streams, there will be salt lakes at the end of these creeks or streams – like the Dead Sea.

Ultimately, all water flows into the sea, evaporates there under the sunlight, and forms clouds, some of which rain down over the land and then form streams and rivers again. This water cycle has greatly shaped the surface of the earth and is also the basis for plant, animal and human life on land.

Water also shapes the earth where large amounts of water and the land meet such as on riverbanks and the coast. The waves and patterns in the sand are much the same at rivers and at the sea, but the land as a whole is shaped differently. The river meanders through the land, washing away land and washing it back up elsewhere, digging valleys and gorges and carrying away mountains. The sea acts by ebbing and flowing, enlarging all the bays and passages between two seas. The bays are driven further and further into the land and they also become more and more pointed. The islands formed by deposited sand in rivers and off the coast, on the other hand, are elongated-round.

The earth, which is washed by the rivers into the sea, forms partly quite large deltas with many river arms. Whether the rivers form such deltas or whether the sea enlarges a river mouth into a bay reaching far into the land depends on the relationship between the tidal effects and the amount of sand washed up by the river.

An effect of the rivers is also the rounding of the stones into pebbles and the grinding of the stones into sand. When this sand is deposited in calcareous water and remains there for a long time under greater pressure, sediments such as sandstone can form.

Finally, there are the ice volcanoes ("cryo-volcanoes"), of which there are two varieties. One variety is found on Earth in Siberia, and in our solar system on Pluto, Charon, and Ceres. These cryo-volcanoes are formed by water freezing beneath the Earth's surface and exerting a pressure that is sometimes sufficient to force water and ice out the top, creating small hills as well as flat mountains in Siberia. The second variety of cryo-volcanoes is found on the moons Enceladus, Triton, Europa, and Titan. These moons are covered by a thick layer of ice floating on a liquid sea. The ice creates high pressure on the water, which occasionally forces some of the water up through cracks in the ice and can form fountains several hundred kilometers high. These cryo-volcanoes could also be called "ice geysers."

II 7. c) Air

The forms of air cannot be seen at first – air needs another element to become visible.

In fire, air can only move the flames or fan the embers – but this can lead to violent effects in forest fires.

In water, the wind causes waves to form. The wind is also visible in the form of clouds. The carbonic-acid geysers as for example in Andernach at the Rhine originate from the fact that carbonic acid collects in the earth and then by the developing pressure water presses upward by an earth gap. Here it is the air (carbonic acid gas) that creates a geyser.

The wind forms sand in the same way as water – except that sand moves much more slowly than water. Dunes can be thought of as high sand waves. Wind erosion on rocks is also one of the effects of air and so is the growth of trees.

II 7. d) Earth

The primary movement of the earth is the rising hot lava from the earth's interior, which is lighter than the cooled lava at the earth's surface. In most cases it rises to the surface in long fissures. Such a fissure is found, for example, in the Atlantic Ocean, where it extends roughly from the North Pole to the South Pole. The lava rising there forms a long mountain range – the Mid-Atlantic Ridge. Some volcanoes on this ridge are so high that they reach above sea level and therefore appear as islands. Another such rift extends in the North Pacific from Siberia to Hawaii and is recognizable on any map as a long series of volcanic islands. This rising lava appears either as a single volcano (e.g., Vogelsberg near Frankfurt), as a group of volcanoes (e.g., Canary Islands), or as a long series of volcanoes (e.g., in the North Pacific).

One can recognize the relatively young fissures of the earth, at which lava rises, at the earth surface by the fact that there fissures, deep and long valleys, new sea arms etc. develop – like e.g. from the Dead Sea by the Gulf of Akaba and the Red Sea up to Ethiopia – at the soil of the Red Sea one can already recognize the emergence of a new mountain ridge form by rising lava.

The rising of the lava from the earth's interior is like the bubbling water in a cooking pot – only in extreme slow motion.

This rising lava in the long fissures pushes the earth away to its left and right, causing continental drift – the Mid-Atlantic Ridge, for example, pushes America away from Africa/Europe. This results in a second deformation of the Earth: the continents that are pushed across the Earth form a kind of bow wave of earth such as the Rocky Mountains and the Andes on the west side of America, which is pushed into the Pacific Ocean by the Mid-Atlantic Ridge. In these bow waves (mountain ranges) and in front of them there are logically also most earthquakes and many volcanic eruptions.

The third form of the formation of mountains (besides volcanoes and bow wave mountain ranges) are the collision mountains, which are found, where two continents, which are pushed by the rising lava over the earth surface, collide. This is how the Alps were formed between Africa and Europe, and the Himalayas between Asia and India (which was once part of Africa).

The mountains formed in this way are then gradually eroded again, mainly by the rain. In the process, they do not become uniformly flatter, since they contain layers of rock of varying hardness. Therefore, erosion creates long mountain ranges with rows of lakes between them – as can be seen clearly in the Alps, for example.

A rather special earth form are the atolls. These are volcanoes in the sea, which have been gradually eroded by the surf down to sea level, so that finally only a sand island remains on a volcanic foundation.

As last one can also consider the age of a mountain range – e.g. the Scottish mountains are much older than the Alps.

II 7. e)   The importance of the elemental forms

Of course, one does not always have to consider all these influences, but one should at least be able to notice when one of these influences is particularly pronounced. For example, in a house that stands on a volcano, there might be particularly violent quarrels.

It is also well known, for example, that when couples move to the Canary Islands or spend a long vacation there, the "inner fire" of these volcanic islands causes all the things that are otherwise tolerated or swept under the rug to become clearly visible and then lead either to viable solutions or to a separation.

Limestone mountains such as the Dolomites, on the other hand, have a completely different influence than volcanoes: they promote the acceptance of compromises and the building of solid forms.

II 8. The differentiated forms

Besides the rather large-scale natural forms described in the previous chapter, there are also forms that are much more specialized. These forms are also found as "vocabulary" in the crop circles.

These forms result for the most part from the interaction of several forces. If the relation of these forces to each other is the same, also the same forms arise again and again – therefore one can conclude from certain forms to the forces that have shaped these forms.

Of course, these forces do not only appear in the crop circles as single form-elements, but are generally valid and can be found in many areas.

Since I have already described these forms in detail in "Crop Circles for Beginners", here follows only a small excerpt from these form-elements to illustrate this kind of forms and their character.

To these differentiated forms belong of course also the natural forms described in the chapters "II 1." and "II 7.".

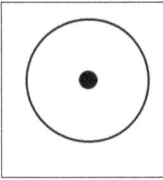

The **unipole** is the simplest form of a crop circle. In it, all elements are arranged concentrically and are therefore to be regarded as aspects of identity. In astrology it corresponds to the aspect of conjunction (0° angle; symbol: ☌), which binds all elements involved tightly together as in a marriage. In nature, this structure corresponds to the unipolar gravity that pulls all things together. It creates cohesion.

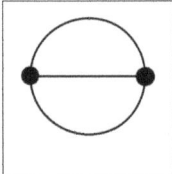

The **two-pole** is a complementary opposition. It consists of two "charges": "+" and "−" or "north pole" and "south pole". It is known mainly by the Yin/Yang symbol (☯), but also by the astrological symbol of the opposition aspect (180° angle; symbol: ☍), both of which describe an eternal change like a swing. This structure corresponds in nature to the bipolar electromagnetic force. It creates attraction and repulsion as well as rhythmic and circular movements.

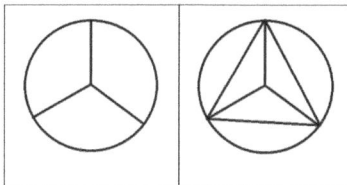

The **three-pole** has three charges, which only together result in the neutral state: "red" + "yellow" + "blue" = "white". In nature it is found as a three-polar "strong nuclear force", which, among other things, shapes the processes in protons and neutrons. Because of the color-metaphor for its three-polarity it is also called "color power". It corresponds to the astrological aspect of the trine (120°-angle; symbol: ▵), which connects all elements involved in a friendship. The three-polarity is also associated with the circular course through several constantly recurring cycles. In astrology, a trine connects the three phases of the same element such as the creating fire of Aries (cardinal sign), the shaping fire of Leo (fixed sign), and the moving fire of Sagittarius (mutable sign).

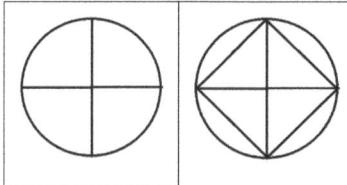

The **quadripole** is found in nature, among other things, between the electric wave and the magnetic wave in a photon – both waves always cross at right angles. In astrology the square separates two things and thereby spans a space (90° angle; symbol: □). The quadripole also corresponds to the four directions with the sun in the center, as well as the four elements with the quintessence in their center. In astrology, the square connects the same phase of the four elements such as the creating fire of Aries, the creating water of Cancer, the creating air of Libra, and the creating earth of Capricorn (the four cardinal signs).

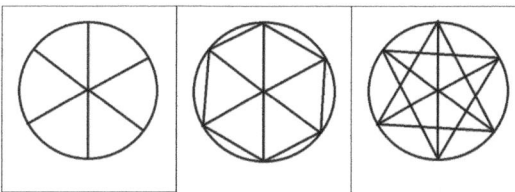

The **six-pole** occurs in many places in nature: as a snowflake, as a honeycomb, as the close position of equal-sized spheres (marbles in a bucket; protons and neutrons in a nucleus), as six moons on the same orbit, all of which have the same distance from each other, and so on. In astrology, the six-polarity is found in the sextile, which binds the same elements together into a group (60° angle; symbol: ✳). This polarity has recently become somewhat better known as the "flower of life". The six-pole, which is a differentiation of the three-pole and thus the interaction of two forces, appears as the more dormant hexagon ("honeycomb") and the more active hexagram ("six-pointed star"). In astrology, the two forces that interact here are either the three phases of fire and the three phases of air, or the three phases of water and the three phases of earth.

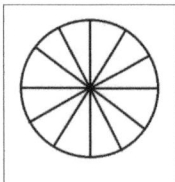

The **twelve-pole** results from the combination of the one-polarity with the two-polarity, the three-polarity and the four-polarity. It is found in nature as the 12 basic elementary particles, as the twelve-part superstring (the basic element of physics today), and as the zodiac. The surrounding space of a center is twelve-divided. This polarity is very common in crop circles.

The **circle**, which is sometimes called "area of a circle" for a better distinction, is a center and therefore the area of identity. He is an individual and therefore also the basic building block of the crop circles, which were at the beginning only such circular areas for a long time.

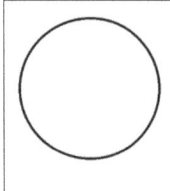

The **ring**, which is sometimes also called "circle", is a surrounding space, an environment, a skin, a city wall, a radiation etc.. It can be static, but it can also rotate or something can flow in it like in a pipe. The ring is often twelve-divided like the zodiac or the superstring, in which also something flows in the circle. This twelve-division is not always drawn into the crop circle as a structure, but this structure is, so to speak, always present in all rings without explicit expression.

The symbolism of the **straight line** is simple: Either it is as a straight line the shortest connection between two points or it is a ray which leads out from a point into the surrounding space.

An **arc** is a part of a ring. These are mostly semicircles, more rarely quarter circles and very rarely three-quarter circles. The semicircle is an opening to something else: a fixture, a transmitter or a receiver – it is like a parabolic mirror. The quarter circle is more like a point of contact. The three-quarter circle is an open vessel.

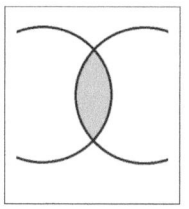

The **almond** is the intersection of two circles. Its long axis is at right angles to the line connecting the centers of the two circles. Thus, the almond lies transversely between two individuals and is shaped by them. It therefore expresses something in common: the area in which two individuals (circles) coincide. One can also look at the almond in a second way: The centers of the two circles exert pressure on each other, creating a flat shape that moves between this pressure – like fish, which are also usually approximately almond-shaped and can most easily move through water resistance with the help of this shape. Which of the two interpretations is more suitable in each case, one must decide from case to case.

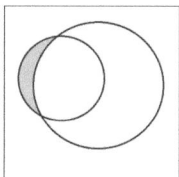

The **crescent** is in a way the counterpart of the almond: it is the part of the area of two circles that is not common to both. Therefore, the crescent is something attached to something else, something that supports or protects something else. It can also be something receiving. The crescent, unlike the almond, also has a clear alignment because it has two different sides: The inner arc receives and seeks contact; the outer arc repels and protects. This form may be found for example as a river delta or an island.

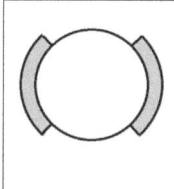

The **crescent circle** has a slightly different meaning than the sickle, since the crescent circle describes an internal process, while the sickle describes an external process. The crescent circle shows that the inner circle moves from the center to the edge – a movement impulse. When several crescent circles appear one after the other, they form a conduit, so to speak, for this movement impulse – they are then both the movement itself and the envelope of this movement. Therefore, a series of crescent circles is also well suited for the representation of dorsal vortices and the like. The circle area with to crescent circles is found for example as the core of an electromotor.

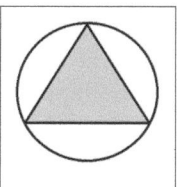

An **equilateral triangle** is a tripole, i.e. the combination of three poles into one unit. The triangle thus stands for a dynamic unit that moves and develops. In crop circles, however, the arc triangle is found much more often than the triangle with the straight sides.

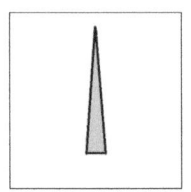

The **pointed triangle** is a ray, an impulse, an attack, a defensive structure, or the like. Its interpretation depends largely on the context in which it appears.

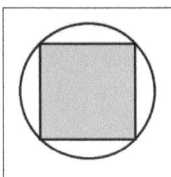

The **square** appears very rarely in crop circles but very often in human culture. It is very static, solid, hard and spans a space. It can therefore be a foundation or a protective wall.

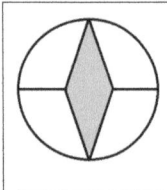

A **rhombus** is a square without right angles or with two diagonals of different length. It appears as an area between two groups of parallel lines. If these lines are straight lines, the classical rhombus with straight sides is created; if these lines are arcs, however, the arc rhombus is created, which will be discussed in the following. Because the rhombus is created as a surface between overlapping parallel lines, it is almost always an indication of force fields, i.e. of the relationship between two impulses that meet.

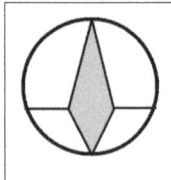

The **pointed rhombus** is a rather rare shape, although it is actually quite interesting. It is created in the same way as the normal rhombus, but also has the quality of a ray, i.e. it has a direction: it moves in the direction of the narrower tip. This form is found in nature also in spikes and thorns.

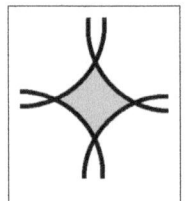

An **arc rhombus** with four arcs pointing inward is called a "diamond". It is created as a space between four circles whose centers form the corners of a square. Thus, the diamond is the space in the center left by four individuals (circles) of equal size (= equal strength) when they span a space. A diamond is thus a shape that is under pressure from all four sides. It tends to implode, that is, to collapse in on itself. This form appears for example if a large hole in the ground is filled with earth in equal measure from four sides.

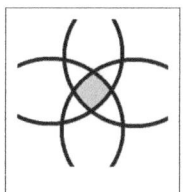
The **arc diamond** with four outward arcs is the common intersection of four circles whose centers form the corners of a square. An arc rhombus is the space formed when the outer lines of these four circles do not reach the center between them. The arc diamond, on the other hand, is formed when the outer lines of the four circles extend beyond their common center. While the arc rhombus is under pressure from four sides, i.e. from the outside, the arc rhombus contains the combined pressure of four circles in its interior, since it is the intersection of four circles. The arc rhombus is thus an extremely expansive element – it is the "anti-square". It works well as the center of a complex shape. It is sometimes found in castle walls.

The arc rhombus, which has two inward arcs and two outward arcs, might be called a "**bud**". The two inward arcs (in the sketch below) make pressure on the bud, which in turn makes pressure outward with its two outward arcs (in the sketch above). So this rhombus of arcs is something that wants to move, that wants to progress, to grow, to come out of something – just a bud, a germ, a penis, an unborn child, a new thought, a strong impulse, the alluvial soil of a stream in a plain, a molehill, etc.

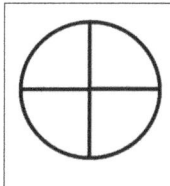
The **cross** occurs relatively rarely in crop circles. It is formed when two lines cross at right angles. Such lines are usually the connection between two poles – so there must be two poles twice in a cross.

This is the case e.g. with a photon, which is physically an electromagnetic wave. If you look at such a wave from the front, and if the light comes flying towards you and you would be able to recognize this light in its structure, you would see the following picture: The electric wave, for example, could be the horizontal line – since it is a wave, it would be constantly changing back and forth from the "+" on one side to the "–" on the other. The magnetic wave would then be the vertical line and would be constantly changing between the "north" at one end and the "south" at the other end from up to down and back. The proportion between these two waves is always a right angle (90°). This angle is the maximum distance between the four poles involved. Such a cross is therefore a very stable proportion.

Also in astrology, the 90° aspect ("square") is a very stable angle that spans a space. So a cross is rigid, solid, stable and gives rise to forms that have two longitudinal axes.

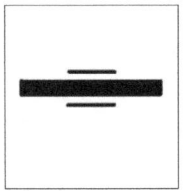 The **companion pair of lines** seems to be something like a shell, i.e. a line. In crop circles these lines almost always appear in pairs – to my knowledge only next to straight lines, but not next to arcs. This suggests that they also have the function of aligning the straight line between them. They are, so to speak, what makes a normal light beam become a laser beam. This is usually avoided in Feng Shui, for it creates "hard life force".

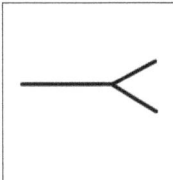 The **line bifurcation** is extremely rare and appears only on two crop circles, which are also so inaccurately made that one might suspect that they were created by humans. If this bifurcation has the angle of 90° or 120°, it could have a meaning – just the space creation (90°) or the binding to a unit (120°). In human culture this form shows a division or a merging of forces – for example the current flow in a conduction or the traffic on a road.

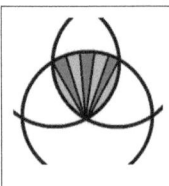 The **feathers** are often indistinguishable from rays – what is meant by these elongated shapes can often only be seen from the context. But since they are either the representation of a movement (ray) or what causes a movement (feathers), this distinction is not very important, since this form indicates a movement in both cases.

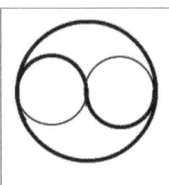 The **"S"** is formed on the outer edge of two polar circles and is also an element found in the Yin/Yang sign. It represents a tension and a movement.

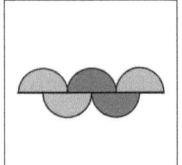 The **semicircle series**, i.e. a straight line with semicircles on either side, each end of which meets the center of the semicircle on the other side, is a second way of constructing an "S" (the single dark gray shape). Here a longer movement is shown than with a simple "S". Therefore, the semicircle series can also be seen as a sequence of several "S".

The **snake line** is nothing else than a semicircle series, where the inner angles between the semicircles have been rounded. It also represents a longer movement. This is for example the form of flowing water – as a river and also as the patterns in the sand at the coast.

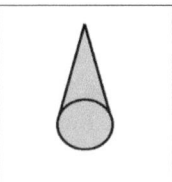

The **straight drop** is the movement of a circle in a certain, straight direction – thus the "falling" or "being pulled" towards something else.

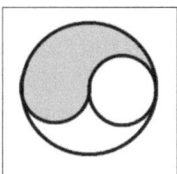

The **curved drop**, also called "miribota", is also a movement, but in a circle. Such a movement occurs when the impulse of the drop (which would move it in a straight direction) is joined by an attraction from the side. This principle is found e.g. in the circular orbits of the planets around the sun or of the electrons around an atomic nucleus. The Yin/Yang sign also represents this principle. The Miribota thus indicates the movement of a unit (circle) within a system. In most cases, this system consists of two units: the two polar circles representing "+" and "–", "north" and "south", yin and yang, and so on. These two poles revolve around each other, giving rise to the movement of the curved drop.

The **spiral** is either a development from inside to outside or a development from outside to inside. Here the ray is superimposed with a circular movement. So one can conclude from a spiral that the system in question radiates, i.e. expands or shines, and that the system in question rotates, i.e. rests in itself – or that the system rotates and shrinks.

The **symmetrical double spiral**, which is also known as the Chinese luck symbol, is created when an impulse enters a system. This is the case, for example, when a stream flows into a pond (right sketch). In the sketches the impulse comes from below. This form can be found in many places like for example in the ovaries of a woman (left sketch). The symmetrical double spiral is formed in the system where an impulse enters – the impulse itself takes the form of the "bud", which is found, among others, in the penis of the man (middle sketch). The bud and the symmetrical double spiral thus belong together and are the two forms which arise when two systems connect with each other (right sketch).

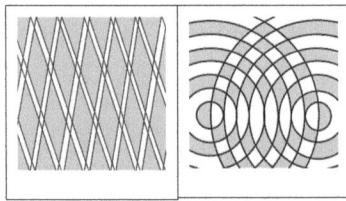

The **force field of rhombuses** results from the super-position of parallel straight lines or arcs, which again are waves emanating from an active center. These centers are usually circles (right sketch). By superimposing the concentric circles starting from two different points or the rows of straight lines starting from two straight surfaces (left sketch), a pattern is created in which these lines cross each other. This results either in rhombuses with straight edges or in arc rhombuses ("buds").

The rhombus pattern thus represents a force field in which the influences of both "transmitters" are combined and graphically represented. The shape of the rhombuses depends on four influences:
1. the number of transmitters,
2. the shape of the transmitters,
3. their distance from each other, and
4. the considered section of the common force field.

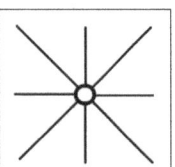

The **lines starting from a center point** represent a radiating, expanding system shaping its surrounding space.

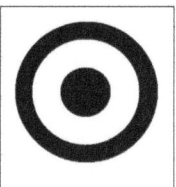

The **circular area with a ring** is an individual that has protected itself well. However, the impression of this structure depends very much on the size of the circle, the thickness of the ring and the distance between them. This is for example a tower with a castle wall or a cell with cell membran and nucleus.

The **small central circle area in a large circle area** centrates this area and gives the impression of consciousness and determination.

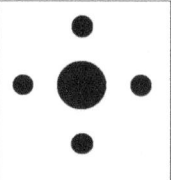

The **central circle with 4 circles** is a center with an organic surrounding space: the sun with the four directions, the quintessence with the four elements, etc. So this form is a structured organism.

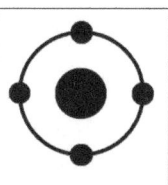

The **central circle with ring and 4 circles** corresponds to the previous form. It is however more stable becaus of the ring and it is outwardly delimited. Therefore, almost only this form occurs in crop circles – the previous, ring-less form is extremely rare. This may be a tower, a castle wall and four turrets.

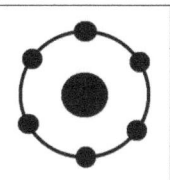

The **central circle with a circular ring and 6 circles** is even more organic than the two previous forms, because the "6" represents an organic group and not only a space like the "4".

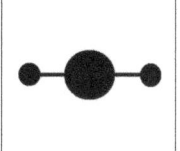

The **center circle with two pole circles** is, so to speak, the motor or the heart of very many crop circles. The two poles cause the pulsation or rotation of the central circle – like an electric motor or a heart. This form can also be seen as a magnet or a battery.

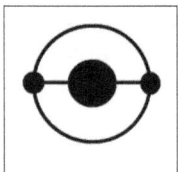

The **central circle with two pole circles and ring** emphasizes the unity of the system by the ring. The ring also represents the rotation and pulsation of energy in the system.

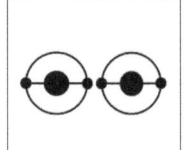

The **rows of polar circles** that sometimes occur in crop circles are, so to speak, magnets, batteries or electric motors connected in series, which together have a greater force than a single polar element. This structure occurs almost only in the long crop circles.

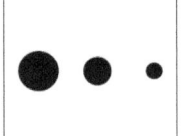

In the case of **triple shapes with decreasing or increasing magnitude**, in addition to the cycle, a direction is emphasized in which this cycle develops. Again, circles are most often used.

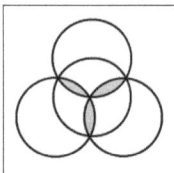

The **almond three-star**, like the previous two forms, is indicative of an unfolding, a development, or a cycle. This three-star is created by the intersections of three circles whose centers lie on a fourth circle. This structure emphasizes the radiance of the cyclic system.

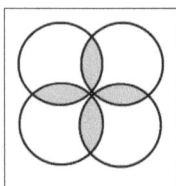

The **almond cross**, on the other hand, according to the symbolok of the "4", emphasizes the occupation, conquering and shaping of a space.

The **Almond Six Star** emphasizes the organic design and coordination of all elements with each other in this radiating system.

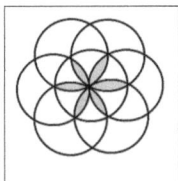

The **almond six-pointed star** with central circle distinguishes the center from the surrounding space of this structure. This form is also called the "flower of life". It is also the representation of the sextile aspect in astrology (60° angle), which describes an organic group formation.

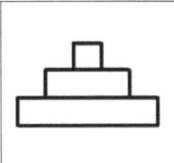

The **step pyramid** is in principle a layered triangle and therefore has the same symbolism as a triangle. However, it appears more stable and the cycle aspect recedes into the background. Therefore this form is rather a defense bastion than an indication of a development.

Dot rows are paths, indications of connections, rays and the like. They are rather unspecific, because they only represent a general connection, but don't have a certain quality or direction.

7-point rows, which often have a slightly larger central circle, are a representation of the chakras: the center (heart chakra) unfolding upwards and downwards in a three-step process – impulse (solar plexus, throat chakra), structure (hara, third eye) and contact (root chakra, crown chakra).

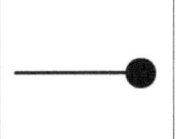

Endpoints on lines simply end a straight line, which would be a ray without that endpoint at that end. While a ray goes out from a center endlessly into the distance, a straight line starts at a center (circle) and ends at another center.

II 9.   Direct Perception

The methods presented so far have all been analytical, i.e. a place has been observed and from what is seen, the forces have been inferred which have caused the place to look just as it does. From the physical form of a place, th physical forces, that have been shaping this place, were first inferred and then it was assumed that the life force corresponds to these physical forms and their character.

However, there are also methods of directly perceiving the life force and thus the quality of a place. They are presented in the three following subchapters.

II 9. a)   Riding the Dragon

This is a traditional intuitive method from Feng Shui. First you walk in a wide circle around the place you want to examine. Mark all the places where you feel more power than at the other places on this circle. Then you stand at one of these places and just spontaneously start running to the inside of this circle and then mark the way you have been running. Then repeat this with all other places on the circle.

In this way, at the place you are examining, you get a network of lines where more life force flows than at other places – the life force directs your own spontaneous run path at that place. With the help of this network of lines, one can then see where the power places are in that place – where several of the lines cross.

The life force that flows along this line is personified as a "dragon" in China. (There are primarily earth dragons, water dragons, and cloud dragons, as well as the golden sun dragon, which is the emperor's life force, among others.)

Next, the power places found in this way can be looked at more closely to describe their character – their strength is determined by the number of lines that cross at it, as well as their location in relation to the other power places. These power places, where several "dragon paths" cross, could also be called "dragon nests".

The life force map of this place, that is created by this method, is afterwards the basis e.g. for the design of the house, which one wants to build at this place.

Of course, one should practice this method a bit before using it as a basis for concrete planning.

If you have the possibility, you should have three or four people do this method independently and then compare the results. In this way one can achieve a somewhat greater certainty in the results.

This method is closely related to family constellations. The only difference is that one does not translate one's perceptions of the life force into gestures and words, but into movements (runs = "riding the dragon").

II 9. b)   Dream journeys

This is an internal-direct method. One sits down at the place in question or in front of a map on which this place is marked and looks around inwardly at this place, i.e. one makes a dream journey to this place. With a little practice one can recognize in this way most of the qualities of the place in question.

Here, too, it is advisable, at least with larger projects, to let several persons do such a dream journey independently of each other and then to compare the results afterwards and to examine the possibly differences in the results more exactly, in order to arrive at a description of the place as reliable as possible.

In dream journeys, the perceptions of the life force are not translated into gestures and spoken words (family constellations) or into movements (dragon ride), but into inner images and inner words.

Other similar methods are dowsing and pendulum. In both cases a tool is used as a "monitor" for the perceptions of the life force – either the dowsing rod or the pendulum, the movements of which are caused unconsciously by the arm and hand muscles of their user. Since the meanings of these movements have been predetermined, the sub-consciousness of the subject is able to communicate its own telepathic perceptions to the waking consciousness through these dowsing rod or pendulum movements.

I have described this complex field in detail in my book "Auto-Movement for Beginners".

II 9. c)   Clairvoyance

This is an external-direct method. Basically it is very similar to a dream journey, except that in clairvoyance a different projection surface is used for the perceptions – one experiences the perception not as an inner image, but as an image projected onto the physical environment.

This clairvoyance may consist of spots in the place that begin to glow. It also happens that colored schemes and figures appear at the place. Rather unspectacular, on the other hand, is the spontaneous "knowing" which spot has which quality in that area.

- - -

These three direct methods of perception all require a little practice, but can then be a great enrichment of the analytical method, which concludes from the concrete place to its quality.

II 10.   Examples

The way of perception of the quality of a place is different for each person – after all, everyone has his own biography, his own horoscope and his own experiences. Therefore, in a book one can only give suggestions – which of course are very much influenced by the character of the author.

One can try to reduce this one-sidedness by using as many known methods as possible in the examples and also by using as many different examples as possible.

In the end, everyone must find his own method, since he will be most effective with this individual method.

II 10. a)   The Earth

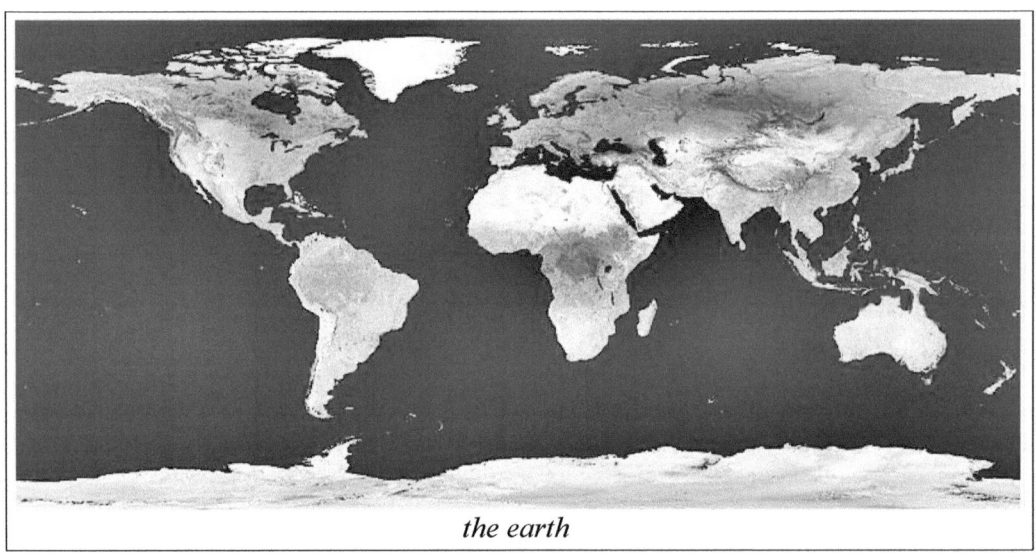

the earth

This is the largest possible place that can be considered on the earth – just the entire surface of the earth. Of course, this is only possible as a description of the large areas.

First of all, you can see that America is pushed westward by the Mid-Atlantic Ridge and therefore forms a long-drawn mountain range on its western side (left) – this is the unstable side of this continent, where mountains pile up, earthquakes shake the earth, and volcanoes erupt. The eastern part of North and South America is largely flat and crossed by large rivers – this half is calmer, wetter, more peaceful.

It is easy to see on the map how North and South America originally hung together with Africa and Europe as one large continent before being forced apart by lava rising at what is now the Mid-Atlantic Ridge. Since America is smaller than Africa/Eurasia, especially America has been pushed away and consequently formed a "bow wave mountain range" on its western side. Before this continent separation and the formation of the American west mountains, the today's Congo flowed on through the riverbed of the Amazon and has then flowed into the Pacific – by the formation of the west mountains the Amazon has had to change its flow direction.

Africa is in a certain way the "old continent" – many ancient and large animals are found here and the first humans (Homo erectus) as well as today's humans (Homo sapiens) originate from here. In addition, Africa was the middle piece of the former large continent Gondwana, before this has divided into today's continents. Africa is so to speak the "heart of the continents".

Antarctica, India and Australia were once located on the eastern side of the lower half of Africa.

Antarctica has drifted south and has gradually iced over.

Australia has drifted eastward and has developed quite a distinct fauna and flora.

India has drifted to the northeast and eventually pushed against Asia, piling up Tibet and the Himalayas. These mountains are still growing the fastest today, but at the same time are being eroded by the rains. That is why this is the "most upcoming place" on earth – it is probably no coincidence that it is here that the Tibetan Buddhist religion was formed.

South of the great mountains Asia is warm and humid, north of the great mountains humid and cold. The same is true in a mitigated form for Europe.

The Alps are a fairly recent mountain range, formed by the collision of Africa and Europe.

The equatorial strip of the earth is humid and hot – here the tropical primeval forests grow. North and south of it lie the two dry zones, which are much larger in the northern hemisphere (Sahara to Gobi) than in the southern hemisphere (Kalahari), because by far the largest part of the land mass lies in the northern hemisphere of the earth.

These two dry zones are followed by two wet zones in the north and south, where the boreal forests of Eurasia and North America grow.

Finally, in the far north and south lie the two ice regions: Arctic and Antarctic.

II 10. b)   A continent

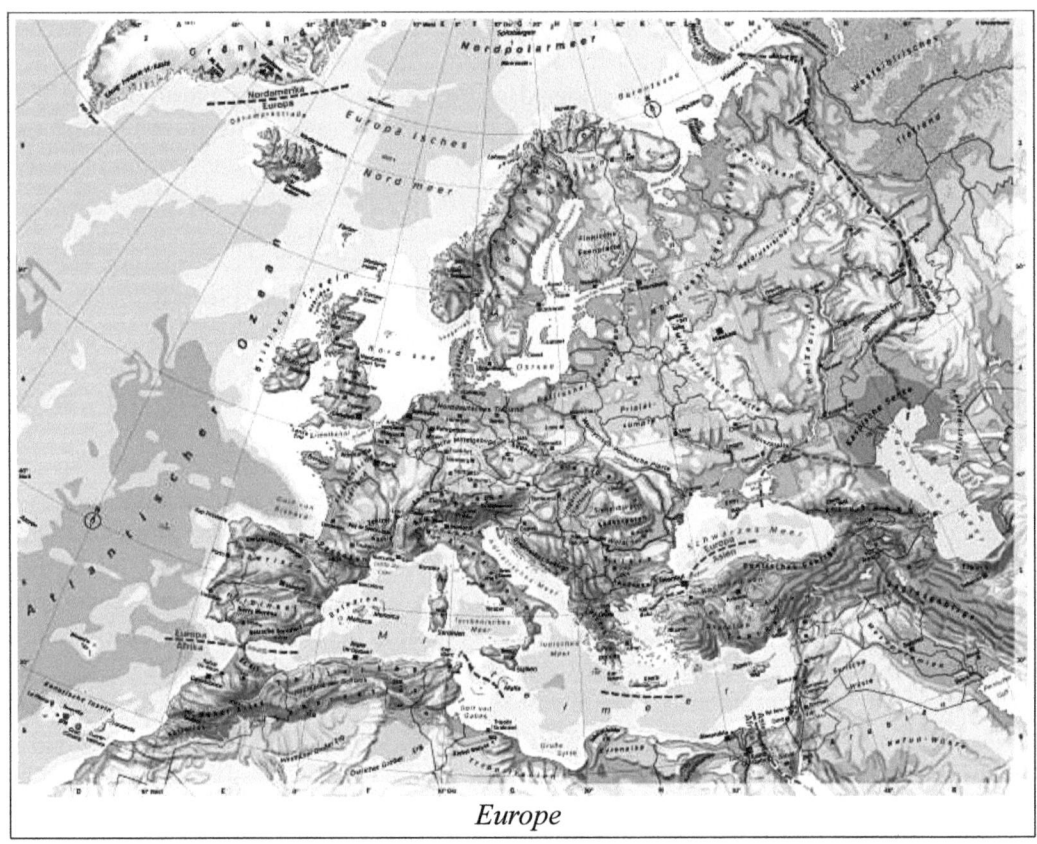

Europe

From the point of view of the history of origin, Spain/Portugal did not originally belong to the European continent, but was an independent island. The Pyrenees were formed by the impact of this island on Europe.

Great Britain and Ireland are separated from the rest of Europe by shallow seas only since the end the last ice age.

The mountains in Scotland are the oldest known mountains – so this should be a place with "deep roots" and great backing.

The mountains in Scandinavia rise in elevation by about 1cm per year. This is because this area has been covered by a 3km thick layer of ice during the Ice Age, pushing the land down – which is now gradually "resurfacing" in the 12,000 years since the Ice Age ended.

While the Mediterranean, Baltic and Black Seas are three "calm seas" because they are inland seas, the effect of high and low tides on the North Sea is very great, causing the mostly flat coastline to be mote and more eroded. As a result, the northern coasts of Germany, Holland, Belgium and, to some extent, France are "vulnerable areas" that are very much under the influence of the sea.

II 10. c) A country

FRG

The basic dynamic in Germany is the north/south slant: the mountains in the south and the flat coast in the north. Therefore, most rivers flow from south to north – only the Danube flows from west to east.

One prominent area is the Alps, which are much younger (and therefore still higher) than the other mountains in Germany.

Another striking feature is the Upper Rhine Valley, which was formed when Africa collided with Europe, creating a rift in southern Germany. Therefore, there is a large volcano in the south of this rift (Kaiserstuhl) and also in the north of this rift (Vogelsberg). Through the rift in the earth's surface the lava could rise more easily to the surface at this place.

Another volcanic area is the Eifel. This area extends in several places even beyond the Rhine to its eastern side. This volcanism has led, among other things, to many carbonated mineral springs in this area as well as to the carbonated geyser in Andernach at the Rhine.

The Swabian Alp, the Franconian Alp and the Black Forest separate the catchment area of the Danube from the catchment area of the Rhine, the Weser and the Elbe. The Danube valley is thus an independent area in terms of water symbolism, while the rest of Germany is largely a unit of parallel flowing rivers in this respect.

In addition to the fire symbolism of the volcanoes and the water symbolism of the rivers, there is also the wind symbolism of the air. The strongest winds are in northern Germany at the coast, because the winds over the sea are not moderated by mountains.

From the earth symbolism there are roughly three different areas: the earth-fire area of the volcanoes, i.e. above all the entire Eifel; then the flat alluvial area in the north of Germany, which is earth characterized by water; and finally the mountainous area in the center and south of Germany, which is subdivided by many hills and valleys into a large number of small, independent areas.

II 10. d) A landscape

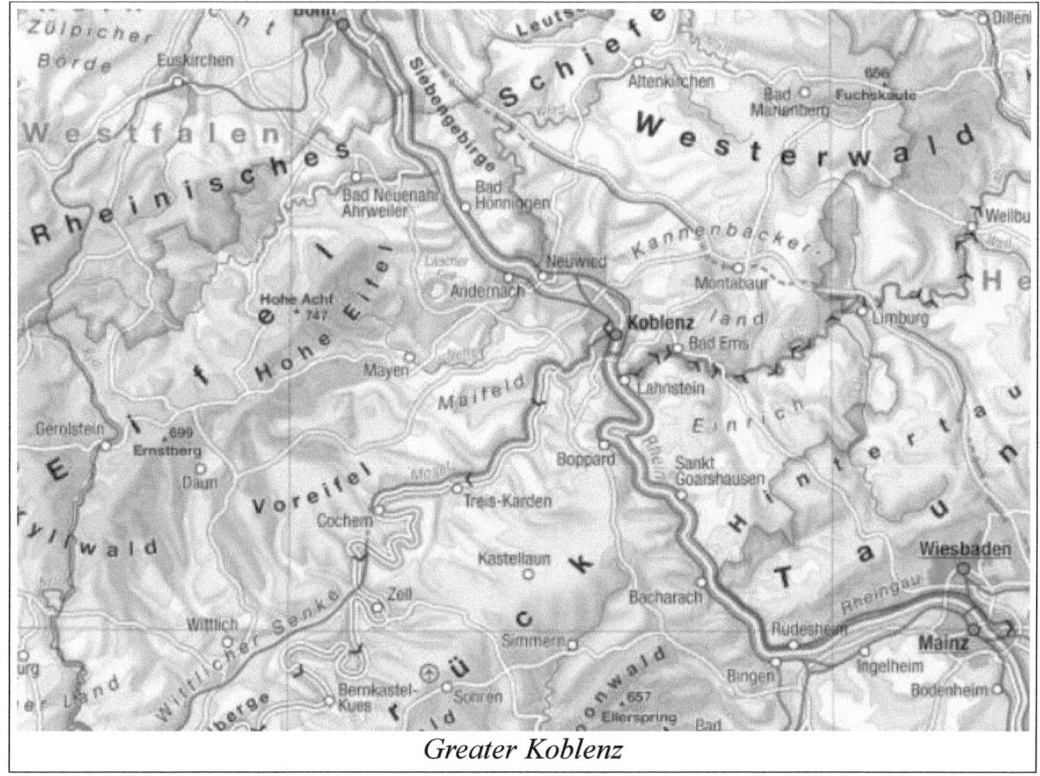

Greater Koblenz

Koblenz is located at the confluence of the Rhine and Moselle rivers. The city is situated on the headland between the two rivers and is consequently surrounded by water.

From Mainz to Koblenz, the Rhine has carved a deep, narrow valley into the mountains there, the northern half of which was formed by volcanic activity in the Eifel region. Shortly after these volcanic eruptions, which ended only 13,000 years ago, i.e. at the end of the Ice Age, the Rhine was dammed up to a huge lake at least as far as Mannheim in the entire Upper Rhine Valley, before the Rhine had cleared its way again.

The volcanism in the Eifel also gives Koblenz a fire quality that comes to the city from the northwest. Just south of Koblenz is Andernach with the aforementioned carbonated geyser – this is an air/water influence.

The other three mountains, Hunsrück, Westerwald and Taunus, are much older and have a calmer influence. In the Taunus there is the Vogelsberg volcano, but this is quite far away from Koblenz.

Koblenz is also a valley town – it is surrounded by mountains all around. South of Koblenz there is a small plain in the Rhine valley, which is a miniature rift valley, which is still earthquake-prone today – this is a restless influence.

II 10. e)   A City

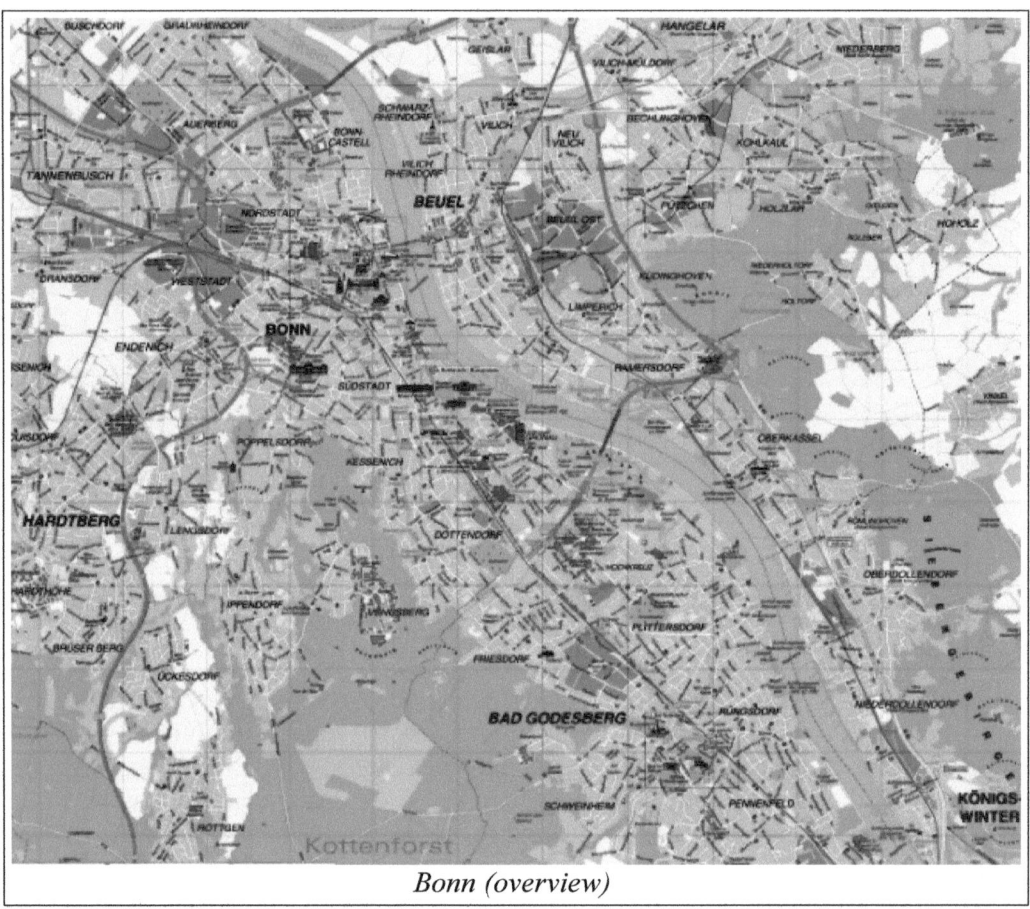

Bonn (overview)

Bonn is located where the narrow Rhine valley widens to the plain that reaches the North Sea. So this city is situated at a transition. Thus, a more or less creative tension is to be expected. The city stands on alluvial land, is surrounded by forests in the east, south and west, in the southeast the volcanic Siebengebirge ("Seven Mountains") lies in sight, and it is flowed through by the Rhine, whose course in the city is bent towards the city center, so that the life force of the Rhine "feeds" the city center. This diversity of the environment increases the creative possibilities in this city. The vitality of the Rhine will still be quite high in Bonn, as it has previously flowed 100km through the narrow volcanic Rhine valley, charging itself with fire energy there, so to speak.

Directly north of Bonn, the Sieg flows into the Rhine, but this has hardly any influence, since the mouth of the Sieg lies downstream from Bonn.

The city has three centers due to incorporations: the center of Bonn, the center of Bad Godesberg and the center of Beuel – so the city is decentralized at least in terms of its layout, which in turn speaks for creative diversity.

The creativity of this city can be seen in the large university, which offers an exceptionally large number of subjects, and also in the many artists, scholars, politicians, etc. who have lived in this city: Ludwig van Beethoven, Robert Schumann, Konrad Adenauer, August Macke, Klara Schumann, Willy Brandt, Hermann von Helmholz, Karl Simrock, Peter Lenné, Hans Riegel (Haribo = "Hans Riegel Bonn"), Paul Kemp, etc.. Moreover, despite its relative smallness (Bonn without incorporations: about 180,000 inhabitants), it has been the German capital for 41 years.

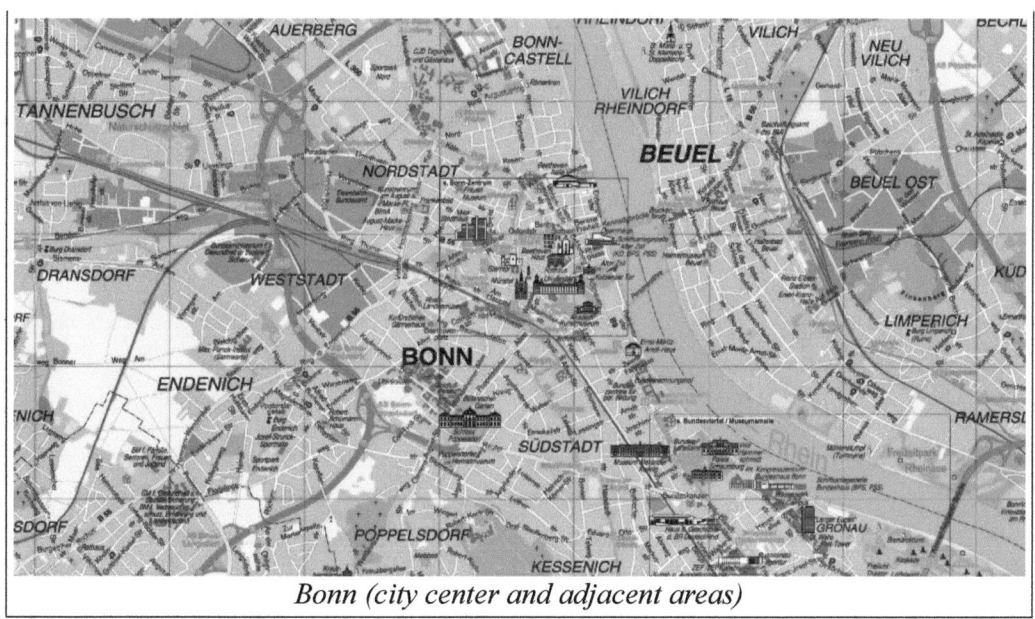

Bonn (city center and adjacent areas)

The city center is located directly in front of the Rhine bend. Bonn and Beuel are separated by the Rhine, but connected by a bridge. Nevertheless, both parts of the city are experienced by Bonn residents as separate entities – the river is stronger than the bridge.

To the east of Bonn's city center is the Rhine, to the north are new housing developments (with a bad reputation) and industrial areas, to the west is the Kottenforst and to the south is Bad Godesberg. Both the city center of Bonn and the city center of Bad Godesberg have many old houses – mostly Art Nouveau buildings. In Bonn there is also the large baroque palace, which is now used as a university, with its large parks.

So Bonn has a great diversity also in its structure: a stylish old center, which is a center of scholarship, in the south a quite similar city (Bad Godesberg), in the east the Rhine (water influence), in the west the forest (connection to organic forms) and in the north rather a "shadow" (new building areas, industry). The respectable inner city is also separated quite precisely by the highway from the less respectable outer areas.

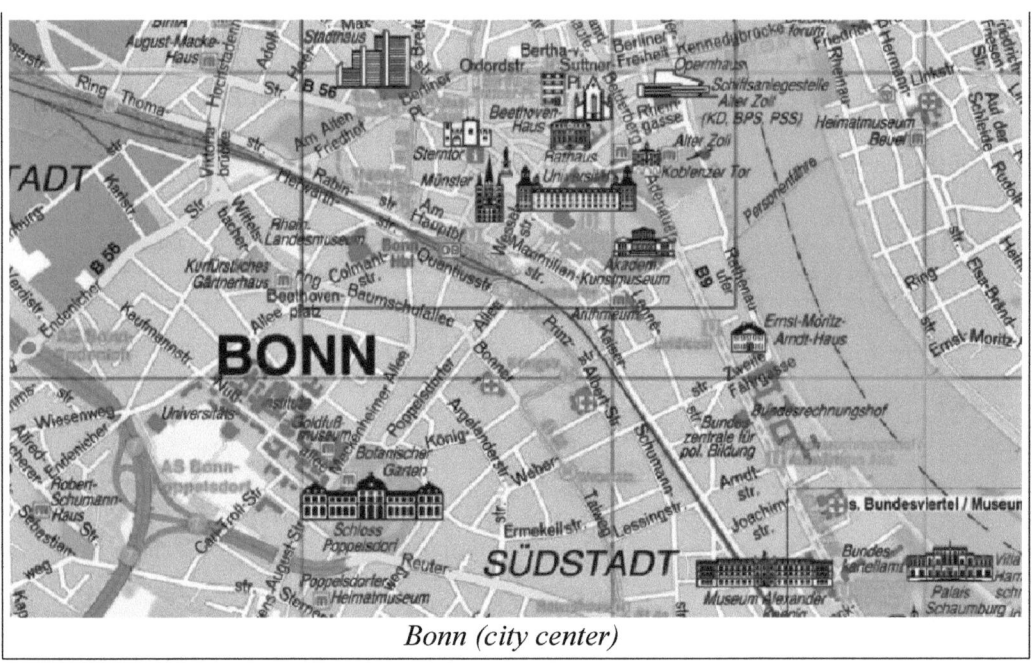

Bonn (city center)

The centerpiece of Bonn is the palace, which consists of two parts: the larger building on the Rhine, from where a long and wide avenue with meadows leads to a second, smaller building. A park is attached to both buildings – the park at the second building is a large botanical garden. Regardless of all other buildings and squares in Bonn, this avenue is the main axis of the city, which also gives it a certain concentration.

II 10. f) A plot of land

The cases considered so far are very rare in the concrete considerations of Feng Shui. However, these considerations give the possibility to see the properties, houses and rooms, with which one usually has to do in Feng Shui, in a larger context and thus to understand the "energetic background" of e.g. a property.

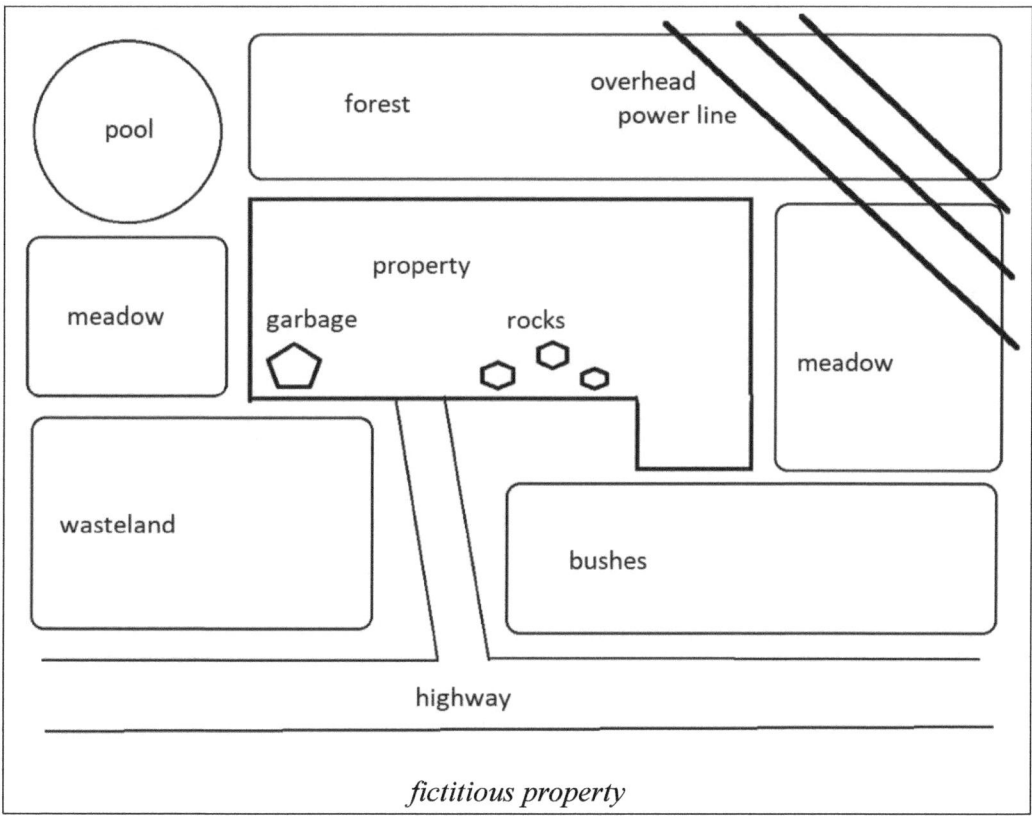

fictitious property

First of all, this plot of land is much wider than it is high – so it will be more of a place for resting than for "aspirational activities". This is reinforced by the fact that the area to the lower right is enlarged by a small amount and thus emphasized – the area of rest, relaxation, letting go.

The access path does not lead straight towards the property, but slightly diagonally to the left, i.e. into the area of the past – this will also lead to this being a place for resting rather than a place for large projects. So it would be awkward to want to build a, say, research lab or strategic planning center here.

The access road branches off from a highway – so it leads from hustle and bustle to tranquility.

To the upper left, outside the property, is a pond. This means that there is a standing water in the place from which the promoting influence comes from the past. A standing water as a promoting influence speaks again for a place of relaxation. For example, one could build a sauna here, or a forest cafe, or a monastery.

Below the property there is the highway and then wasteland and bushes. Above the property, on the other hand, there is forest. So the development from the bottom to the top of this property goes from rushes and wasteland to the property to forest. The two meadows to the left and right of the plot also fit well into this sequence. Obviously, this plot is located in a place where the activities aim at gradually transforming the hectic (highway) into organic forms (forest).

However, high voltage power lines run along the upper right a short distance from the property. This will probably mean that the area of the aims (upper right corner of the plot) will have difficulty unfolding. Without these lines, the quality on the property would be much better …

On the property itself, in the lower left corner, there is a pile of garbage. On the lower left is the place of learning, practicing and efforts. So this plot has not been used for a long time and its potential has not been exploited. Is this because of the power lines that prevent the aims from being reached at the opposite corner?

Finally, there are three rocks at the bottom center of the property. Since the area at the bottom center represents the profession and the general foundation, these rocks give support to the owner of the property. The number of three suggests that it is an organic hold (astrology: trine).

II 10. g) A house

The contemplation of an already existing house might be the most common case one has to deal with in Feng Shui.

To get a first impression, one can compare the house along the vertical axis to the body of a human being:

- The basement is the root chakra,
- the living room is the heart chakra and
- the roof is the head.

Next, you can look for conspicuous features and ask yourself what they might signify – such as:

- a glass roof ("open to the top = inspired"),
- a particularly large bathroom, (cleanliness, enjoying water),
- a huge oil tank in the basement, the filling of which is enough for four years of heating (fear of cold or similar)
- three basement floors (deep anchoring, large root chakra, hidden things?),
- several trapdoors (no direct access),
- several staircases (strong vertical connection),
- a saint figure above the entrance (protection),
    etc.

It is also useful to look for things that are not as they should be:

- a gloomy, oppressive basement (old building?),
- an empty niche for a statue of a saint (lack of protection),
- old posters stuck to the wall of the house (disfigured appearance),
- a broken door (no demarcation),
- a leaky door between the garage and the hallway, through which the car exhaust fumes enter the house (no delimitation, no respect for health),
- an extremely steep staircase, hardly accessible for children and old people (inaccessible areas in the house),
- many passage rooms (unrest, bad usability),
    etc.

You can also lay a Tarot card for each room – preferably on a sketch of the house. This also gives a good first impression, although Tarot cards usually show only how things ae just now.

Also the assignment of the sides of the house to the four elements can give some suggestions (north = earth; east = air; south = fire; west = water).

Finally, one can also look at the individual floors of the house with the help of the Ba Gua – the Ba Gua is only suitable to a limited extent for looking at the house as a whole, since the Ba Gua looks at a surface and not at a three-dimensional structure. However, one can look at the ground plan of a house with the help of the Ba Gua. If the house has a tower or single area that is higher than the others, this area is emphasized as if it had a bulge. You can also draw the peak or ridge of the roof on the sketch and see from where to where it runs.

For plain houses (i.e., most of those built today) this observation is quite simple, but for Art Nouveau houses it is rather complex.

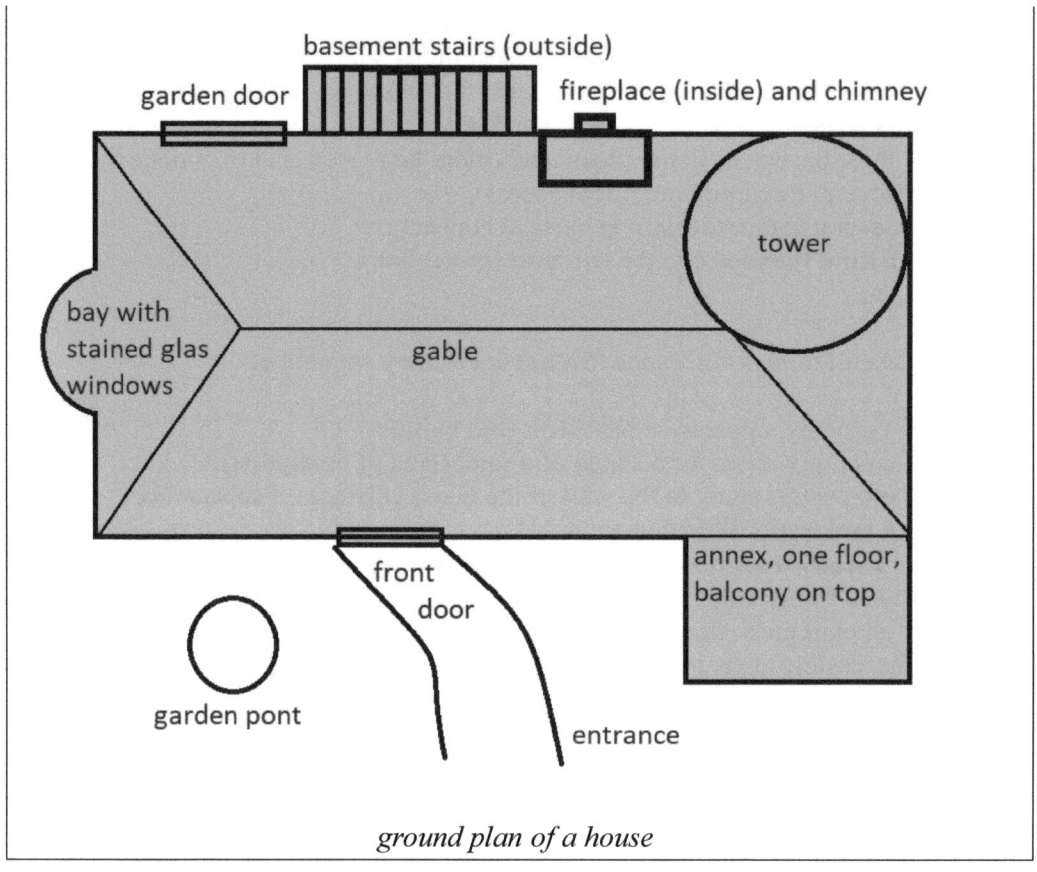

ground plan of a house

The house under consideration has two floors: Basement, ground floor, second floor, roof.

The basic shape is a lying rectangle. Consequently, the house is resting – with the front door on the narrow side of the house, the rectangle would be standing and thus would be much more unstable and restless.

The gable emphasizes the transverse direction, that is, the resting quality of the house. The left and right sloping roof causes a concentration on the center, which will lead to a slightly better focus on the essentials (center of the house) in this house.

The entrance path first leads towards the center of the house, but then turns a little to the left – this is a turning towards the past. Since the entrance is thus between the center/bottom part of the Ba Gua (foundation, occupation) and right/bottom part of the Ba Gua (preparation, learning), this brings a certain restlessness into the house – one is never completely finished, one always has to learn something new, renovate something, change something, and so on.

In addition, the garden pond entices one to linger in the past, i.e. in the learning area – although the water does not particularly stimulate learning, but rather resting …

The semicircular bay window on the left emphasizes the connection to the family of origin (the center/left part in the Ba Gua). Do the people in this house miss their parents? Are they homesick? But maybe the parents and siblings just visit this house quite often.

The area left/top represents the "help from outside". From there a door leads to the garden – is the garden the place where one finds inspiration? On the other hand, help can "flow out of the house" through this door – a door is a opening ater all. Or is this door in invitation to inspiration? Whatever – inspiriation seems to be important to the people in this house.

Furthermore, behind the house and to the right of the garden door are the stairs leading down into the cellar. This stairs were in older houses often located on the outside of the house – does the blessing of the area left/above flow down into the cellar at this place? Ths upper/central part of the Ba Gua is fame and renown – this will not be great in this house … it's going "underground" …

The annex on the lower right emphasizes the area of relaxation, of resting. However, it does not reach up to the roof, but is only single-story. So one is tempted to go from the second floor (heart chakra) to the balcony and relax there in a deck chair with a glass of well chilled OJ …

The tower on the right/above part of the Ba Gua emphasizes the pursuit of a goal, which in many cases will be a happy relationship. This house is quite strongly oriented towards goals.

The open fireplace at the transition from the area above/center (fame, reputation) and above/right (goals, relationships) suggests that these are the areas to which most energy (fire = energy) will be directed in this house.

So on the one hand this house aligns to one's own desires (gable shape) and to one's own goals (tower), but on the other hand it tempts very strongly to relax comfortably (access path, garden pond, balcony) – a house for daydreamers … or a house for people who live their dreams?

One of the most important methods when looking at a house is the dream journey. One goes inwardly through all rooms and feels which quality is to be found here. This is a very helpful method – in this way it is even possible to detect construction defects such as crumbling walls, damp cellars, rotten roof beams and the like. Such a house dream journey can also be made from a distance, if you know the address of the house and then align yourself inwardly with it.

In this way I helped a friend for a while in her search for a house. Of course, one should check everything that one finds on such a dream journey, e.g. construction defects, afterwards with a local inspection – this purposeful search for defects at always precisely the right places will provoke however now and then a little astonishment with the house owners …

With such dream journeys one can determine also things, which cannot be proven physically like e.g. a depressive basic tendency in a room, the presence of a dead spirit, a threatening feeling in the cellar and the like. Sometimes one can get a confirmation for these things by asking exactly – the depressive grandmother may have lived in the room and finally committed suicide, the house may be haunted from time to time, the cellar served as an air-raid shelter during World War II, etc.

These dream journeys can also be simply sitting there, feeling into the place. Since there is an almost unlimited variety of things that can be found especially in older houses, it is not possible to describe all the possibilities in advance. In general, one can say that one should take all perceptions seriously, but not immediately take them at face value, but verifies or falsifies them at the next opportunity …

II 10. h) An apartment

The next smaller unit that can be considered is an apartment or a floor in a house. Here the Ba Gua on the one hand and the dream journey on the other hand are the most important tools – possibly supported by the Tarot cards (one for each room).

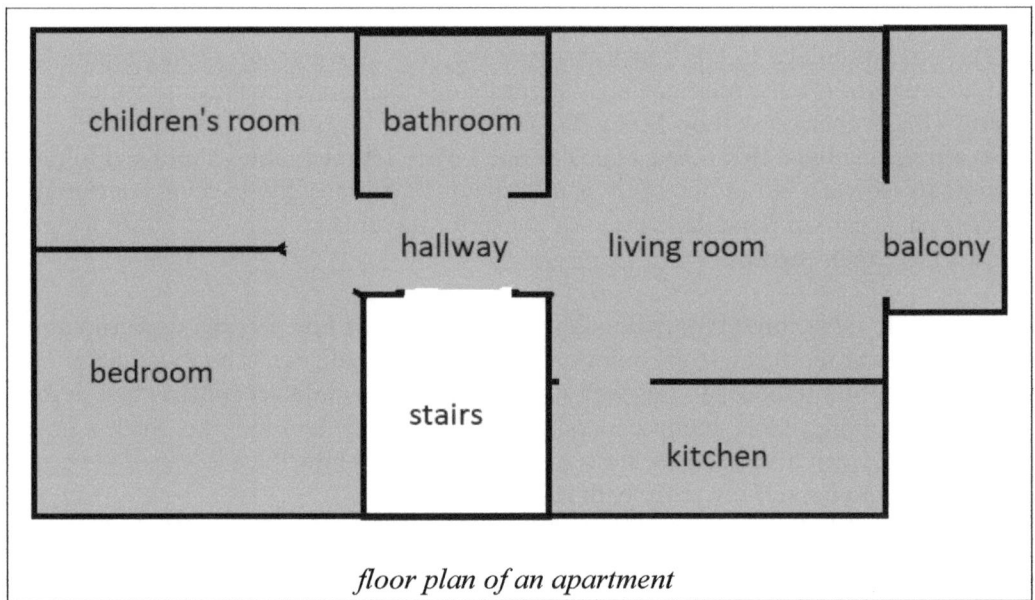

floor plan of an apartment

The staircase is a gap in the apartment – down/centre is the fundament in Ba Gua, the profession, the money-making. Thus, the inhabitants of this apartment may experience a certain lack of support and frequent changes of jobs.

The balcony, on the other hand, is an addition and therefore emphasis on the goals (area on the right/above). The balcony is reached through the door that connects to the area of one's family and creativity (right/center). Probably one will try to reach his goals with the help of his creativity and possibly also try to get money with the help of his creativity and his children. Furthermore, a balcony naturally allows you to look into the far distance – so it will be rather big goals that people pursue in this apartment.

The bedroom is in the area of learning, studying and practicing (left/bottom). It doesn't sound like the occupants are going to get very far on this topic ….

Top left is the "outside help" area – does the family in this apartment live in good part on child support?

The bathroom and WC are where the glory should be found (top/center). The WC probably lets the glory go down the drain, while the bathroom tempts you to rest on your laurels. You're unlikely to become famous while living in this apartment.

At the right/bottom is the kitchen – cooking and eating is thus what you can relax around. That's o.k., as long as eating doesn't become the purpose of life.

Right/top and right/center is the living room – being together with one's own children and one's own creativity (right/center) are obviously the purpose of life (right/top) – which is emphasized by the balcony.

The center of the apartment, where according to Feng Shui the house altar or similar should actually be, is a hallway, i.e. a transit area – the reflection on the essentials should therefore not be so easy in this apartment. After all, the hallway is directly connected to the living room without a door. According to today's building regulations, however, the bathroom would have to have a ventilated anteroom, which could lead to the corridor having to be separated from the living room by a door … which would have the effect of isolating the essential (center) from the everyday life (living room).

If you now lay the tarot cards for this fictitious apartment, you get the following statements:

- <u>Hallway</u>: sword-10, right way up = This card means "self-sacrifice", i.e. probably giving up one's own foundation (area below/middle).
- <u>Bedroom</u>: sword-7, the wrong way around = This card means "robbery with great consequences". So the marriage bed seems to be a trouble spot.
- <u>Children's room</u>: chariot, upside down = This card means "lack of self-realization". The children can't thrive here – because they have to contribute

to the living?

- <u>Bathroom/Loo</u>: king of cups, upside down = This card means "lack of clear recognition and expression of one's desires". In this apartment, people have a hard time showing themselves as they are – the area of fame and prestige is not maintained because there is only the bathroom/toilet.

- <u>Living room</u>: ace of cups, upside down = this card means "lack of feelings, lack of love, depression". The living room, although in the place of ideals, cannot thrive – because you are not really sincere in your feelings.

- <u>Kitchen</u>: lovers, right way around = This card means "lovers, relationship". Is here love replaced by food? Or is the kitchen the place where everyone can relax and you can feel the love for each other again?

- <u>Balcony</u>: coin-6, right way up = This card means "lack of support from outside". Apparently everyone is hoping for better times – but they just won't come.

- <u>Additional card "what to watch out for"</u>: sword-3, upside down = This card means "relationship problems, severe heartache, separation". The problem in this apartment seems to be that relationships cannot flourish here – which is not surprising in view of what has been described so far.

If north is at the top of this apartment, that would be the earth area, that is, thriving. Then material prospering and prosperity would be the thing, an which everything turns in this house, to which everything is aligned and after which everyone strives – this is the element to which everything wants to go upwards. But it does look very much, as if the people in this dwelling live from the social welfare or the like.

Below would be the south, thus fire and thus strength. Well – since by the stairs the whole foundation area (botom/center) is omitted, the foundation of the dwelling and the family is missing strength. The bedroom is also not an area that can implement power well – except perhaps in sex. Only the kitchen can absorb the force somewhat consciously – which could lead to spicy food.

The air would be found on the right, that is, at the future – unfortunately, in view of the considerations so far, this suggests that the future plans are rather airy and not very grounded.

The water is to be found on the left – in the past. So one could assume that the story in this apartment once began with a loving couple who also loved their children.

This apartment is really not ideal …

II 10. i) A room

Almost as often as the contemplation of an entire apartment, the contemplation of one room occurs in Feng Shui.

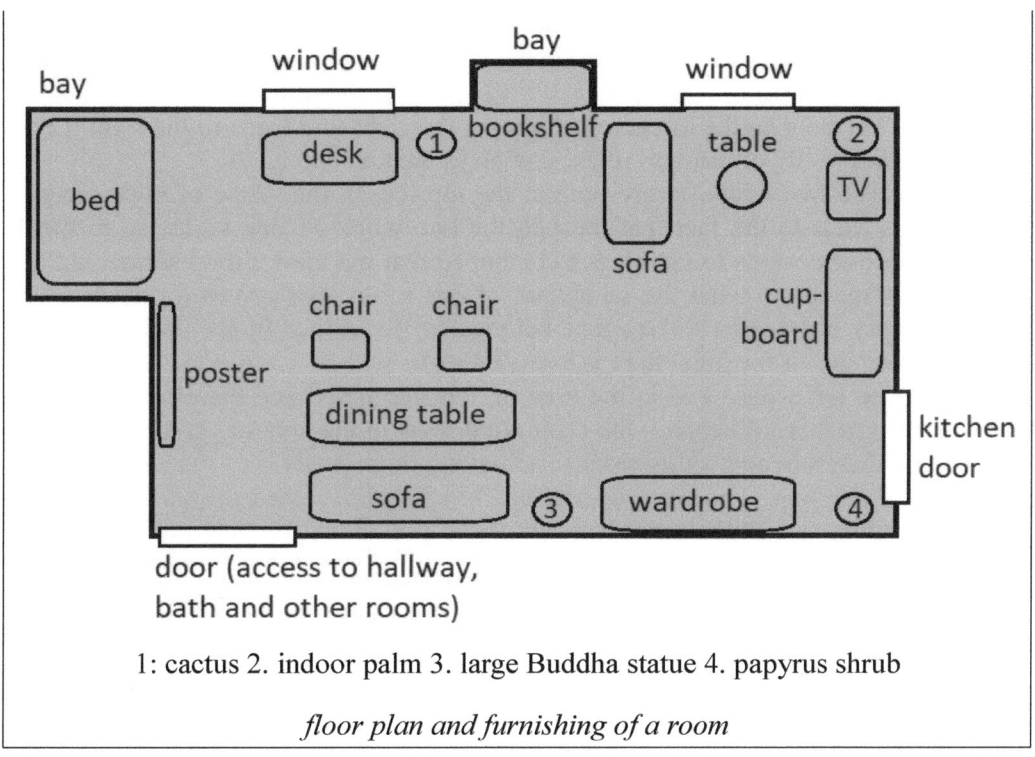

floor plan and furnishing of a room

The floor plan is again transverse, i.e. lying down, and thus tends to be quiet. The floor plan has two peculiarities:

> - The first conspicuous feature is the large bay window at the upper left – if it were any larger (i.e. more than half the wall length wide), it would not be a bay window at the upper left, but a missing part at the lower left. Thus, however, in this room the "help from outside" (top left) is emphasized.
> - The second conspicuous feature is the small bay window at the top center, which is used as a book shelf – here the area of fame and reputation is extended and emphasized. If there is a book shelf there, the erudition of the inhabitant of this room is emphasized – is he perhaps a writer?

The arrangement of the doors and the windows also has a meaning:

- The door to the room is at the bottom left, in the area of learning. This will give this room a bit of a learning and studying imprint. Perhaps there will be meetings of scholars, researchers, study colleagues, etc. here.

Through this door you can also reach the bathroom and toilet, which feels a bit uncomfortable, since the lower left is a very active area and bathroom/ toilet is an area of relaxation.

- The door to the kitchen is down on the right and leads to the right, i.e. to the future: if you want to relax, you go to the kitchen …

- The two windows are both at the top, i.e. in the "zone of high energy". This leads to the fact that through the two windows one looks, so to speak, where one wants to go – it is to be hoped that the view shows something that corresponds to what the inhabitant of this room also strives for, such as the factory premises (if the room belongs to the owner of the factory) or the university (if the inhabitant is a researcher).

The left window is in the area of "outside help" and therefore opens this room to that influence – the right window is in the area of "goals and ideals" and therefore opens this room to achieving those goals.

The remaining part of the room consists of the furnishings, which, unlike what has been described so far, can be easily changed.

- The bed on the upper left: Sleeping in the area of outside help – that doesn't sound ideal, unless you want to receive inspiration in your dreams. This arrangement is reminiscent of the German proverb: "The Lord gives it to his own in their sleep."

- The sitting and eating corner left bottom to left middle: Sitting and eating together is the basis and foundation here – the conviviality obviously serves a common purpose for the people who gather here. The room is a good place for joint projects and for coordination.

- The wardrobe at the bottom right: Clothes as the area of relaxation? Is there careless chaos in the wardrobe or do people have a preference for comfortable clothes? Or both?

- The desk on the upper left: Work is done at this desk possibly to get support from outside or to find a patron. Possibly also religious writings are written here, which are about trust in the gods, or psychological writings about the meaning of primordial trust.

- The book shelf at the top center: The books in the area of fame indicate a learned writer …

- The television sitting area top/right (goals in life): Well – relaxation while watching movies as a goal? This can actually only be productive if the occupant of this room is professionally involved with movies and is possibly a screenwriter. Otherwise, there is a danger that a large part of the energy in this room will be wasted watching TV …

- The cupboard, center/right: The food, for which the dishes are needed, after all, seems to be what the occupant of this room wants to be creative and also representative of – perhaps he also likes to invite his adult children and friends to dinner.

- The cactus at the top center: In the area of fame a cactus … Is the person in this room jealous of the fame of others or is he frugal like a cactus or is he thirsting for glory in an aggressiv way? This is at least a rather difficult arrangement …

- The indoor palm above right: This plant is already a bit friendlier and also grows bigger. By its fanned and "airy" leaves it dissolves tensions – but it also reduces the concentration on the goals and ideals, which correspond to the area on the upper right. This plant fits to the television, which also serves to a large extent the pleasant, shallow dispersion.

- The papyrus at the bottom/right (relaxation): This aquatic plant in the area of relaxa-tion promotes the quality and radiance of this area.

- The Buddha at below/center: The Buddha as a religious figure expresses a general attitude, which has been placed here in the area of the foundation. One may therefore assume that the meetings in this room have a Buddhist or at least in a broader sense religious character.

- The poster on the lower left: A large picture on the wall enclosing the area of learning from the past is likely to have an influence on what is learned here and also on the way in which learning is done here.

This analytical observation would now be followed by a dream journey in the case of a real room or by a feeling into the quality in this room. Thereby one can ask oneself the following questions:

- Where is a lot of energy and where little?
- Where do I like to go and where not?
- Where is the place of highest energy at this place?
- Are there any noticeable qualities in the room? Joy? Depression? Anger? Addiction? Fullness? Hardness?
- Does a person still seem to be present in this room, i.e. is the presence of someone who once lived here still imprinted in this room?
- Does something radiate outwards from this room?

- Is something coming into this room from the outside?
- Is there a distinct connection to other rooms or the like?
- How do the walls, floor, and ceiling of the room feel?
- Do I get the impulse to do something specific in this room?
- Is the spirit of a deceased person present here?
- Is there a distinct connection to something outside the house (tree, river, highrise, railway etc.)?

There are an almost unlimited number of such questions. In the end, however, they are only aids to practice one's own attention a little and to get a feeling for what one could pay attention to.

Again, you can use the Tarot card method if you are unclear about the quality of individual areas of the room or if you have certain questions about the room that you cannot answer with certainty at first.

II 10. j) A table

The same procedure as in relation to a room can be applied to a table, a desk, a cabinet, a shelf, etc. In the case of a cabinet or shelf, one will usually place the Ba Gua vertically – that is, past left, future right, little energy below and much energy above.

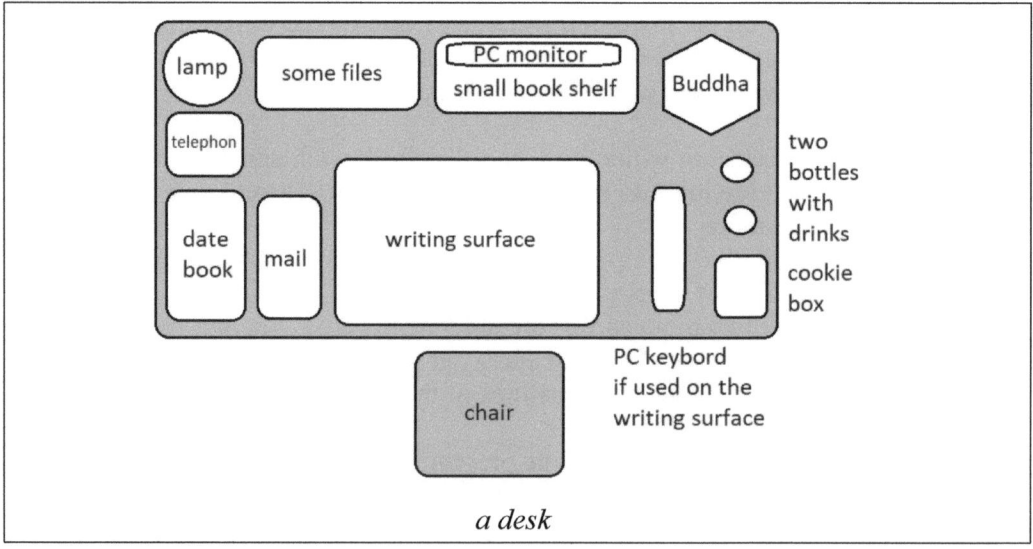

a desk

The chair is in the middle in front of the desk. This is a good position, because it puts it in front of the area "foundation, profession, work" – and this area is what a desk is usually about.

The writing surface is also down in the center and also still covers a large part of the middle area, which is the central theme of an area, which in a desk is usually writing. The writing surface is slightly shifted to the left, suggesting that this desk is more about processing the past than planning the future.

At the top left in the "help from outside" area is the desk lamp – obviously, visibility, clarity and sincerity are important qualities when working at this table.

The telephone is between the far left and the upper left – so one hopes for help from one's relatives and friends (middle/left) as well as from outside, i.e., from a patron or an authority (upper/left).

The diary at the bottom left is the basis of the work at this desk – apparently conversations, phone calls, meetings, appointment work and the like are central to the work at this desk.

The row of folders between top left and top center show that a lot of information is sought after (top/left) and processed into something new and "fame-published" in some way (top/center).

The bookshelf between top center and top right indicates that scholarship and possibly the writing of new books is going on here. The PC monitor on this flat bookshelf suggests that a lot of writing is done on the PC here as well.

The Buddha statue in the upper/left corner in the area of goals and ideals shows which attitude and which topics are concerned with the work at this desk. So it could be the desk in the room that was considered in the previous chapter.

The PC keyboard on the lower right is in the relaxation area. This is also the area where you would put things that you don't need at the moment – like the PC keyboard.

The cookie jar in the area of relaxation shows that the person working at this table does not let himself be stressed and just enjoys himself in between.

The drinks in the center/right in the area of creativity suggest that the person either often takes a creative break or sits at this table with friends or colleagues and drinks and talks, since this area also stands for children and friends.

II 10. k) An object

Looking at a single object with the help of Feng Shui is unusual, but still quite feasible. In most cases this would probably be called "analysis", "contemplation", "telepathy", "psychometry" or "magic" depending on the type of procedure.

For the contemplation of an object according to the method of Feng Shui e.g. the Buddha statue, which stands on the desk in last chapter or in in the room in the forelast chapter, is suitable.

Buddha Manjushri

Buddha Manjushri is the insight aspect of the Buddha: he dissolves all wrong ideas with his flaming sword of realization in his right hand and helps people with the Buddhist scriptures that are on the flower behind his left hand.

Buddha's figure is in the center – he is resting in the here and now.

His head is slightly tilted to the right towards the realm of goals and ideals – he wants to achieve something: Clarity.

He is sitting on a lotus flower, which is in the area of the foundation. The seat of the shamans (from whose tradition Buddha comes) was originally the barrow, which was used as the gateway to the Otherworld – so Buddha is striving for the knowledge of the otherworld, the soul, the fundamental reality.

In his right hand he holds the sword of knowledge, which is in the upper/left area of outside help and in the upper/central area of glory – insight is what changes Buddha. This takes place on the left, that is, on the past side.

The tip of the sword points to tip of the crown chakra – the dissolution of misconceptions by the sword is about recognizing the whole as one (crown chakra).

Behind his left hand is a flower with a book – the Buddhist scriptures summarize Buddha's insights: First the realization (sword, left, past) – then the teaching (book, right, future).

Buddha holds his left hand in the gesture ("mudra") of teaching and explaining – he explains the meaning of the scriptures on the flower behind his left hand.

On the statue, the hara, heart chakra, throat chakra, third eye and especially the crown chakra have been emphasized – it is also about the awakening of the chakras.

The drape in the front between his shins is in the shape of a bud pushing from the inside/back to the outside/front – maybe this could be seen as an indication of the awakening of the root chakra and thus kundalini.

The emphasis on the earlobes by the earrings possibly signifies the hearing of all things.

The pattern on the edge of the robe represents a flow – the flow of life and of the life force.

The strips of cloth on the lower left and right are possibly a reference to Ida and Pingala.

The strips of cloth to the left and right of his body give the impression of space fillers – but maybe thes are indivations of Ida and Pingala, too.

Obviously all the parts of this Buddha statue, that is manufactured in the traditional way, are in accordance with the principles of Feng Shui.

II 11.   The Size of the effect

The question naturally arises as to how great the effect of a place actually is and how great the autonomy and place-independence of man is in a given place.

The answer to this question about the relationship between independence and influence can be approached in three different ways. Some examples are given below, but of course only one's own experience is really convincing.

II 11. a)   Accordances

If several people independently of each other describe a place in the same way, it is very likely that this place really has this quality.

Almost everyone who has described the quality of the organic store "Morgentau" in Alfter, which I co-directed in a collective for 20 years, has called it the "heart of Alfter".

Likewise, just about everyone who has come to the "Hexenhaus" ("witch's cottage") on the edge of Kottenforst (a large forest near Bonn), where I lived for a few years, has said that they feel as if they are on an island in time, as if they are in another world.

 In the Alfter castle, it has been spooking violently for at least a few decades (but probably much longer). It was something that, if you lived there, you couldn't ignore: Invisibles that speak to you at night or pull the covers away from you are hard to displace as illusions …

Volcanic vents like e.g. the Rodderberg near Bonn are generally perceived as power places.

II 11. b)   Differences

The influence that a place has had can often only be recognized when the influence has changed.

Generally one will feel more comfortable in a place after a Feng Shui measure, but sometimes the effect is very obvious – e.g. when one can finally concentrate at one's desk and work comes easily to one.

In the castle of Alfter it has become peaceful since I, together with a friend, sent the spirits into the otherworld and dissolved their imprint on the place.

Sometimes it doesn't take much to make a big impact. For example, I once placed several Flourite crystals at the corners of the office of the organic food store where I worked. As a result, the six people who worked in that office started cleaning up the office and keeping it tidy. This is also exactly the effect of the Flourite crystals, which are cubes and consequently are characterized by the separating, ordering, tidying character of the right angle and the astrological square.

In a fresh, i.e. just newly formed crop circle, almost everyone feels something like an electric tingling, i.e. the high charge with life force. After a few days this tingling in a crop circle fades away almost completely.

Some consecrated objects have an intense radiation. Such consecration can also arise unintentionally – for example, a ring that has been worn by a quarrelsome and jealous woman for 60 years will still carry her character in it after her death. By a purification ritual one can remove this imprint, so that the ring becomes neutral again.

A clairvoyant in Bonn, with whom I once studied, once told me to close my eyes and then put a ring in my hand and asked me to say what quality it had. Since this quality was extremely unpleasant, she asked me if I could clean the ring, which I did. Two months later, I was asked to close my eyes again and feel the quality of what was placed in my hand. This time it was pleasantly neutral – it was the ring I had cleaned.

Religious objects sometimes have an especially strong radiation – for examples the statue of the lion goddess Sachmet in the temple of Karnak or the lines of the statues of Saints around St. Peter's Square in Rom.

Once I cleaned and recharged an old cellar vault that no one wanted to go down into. After that everyone who came into the cellar felt comfortable there and found that it smelled like freshly baked bread and cake – which I also noticed very clearly myself. How this additional "smell effect" came about is completely unclear to me …

II 11. c)   Successes

A rather simple measure of the effect of Feng Shui is its effectiveness. I was once asked by an architect if I could do something to help him find a buyer for a property he had been trying to sell for 20 years.

When we were on the property in question, the cause of the blockage became clear quite quickly. The property was located in the second row behind the properties in the first row at the built-up street and could only be reached with the help of an S-shaped access road that led between the other properties to the second row. In addition, the occupant of one of the two adjacent properties had used the property for sale as an extension of his own garden, so to speak.

This meant that, on the one hand, the plot had the aura of inaccessibility and remoteness because of the S-shaped path, and on the other hand, it also had the aura that it already belonged to someone and was used by someone.

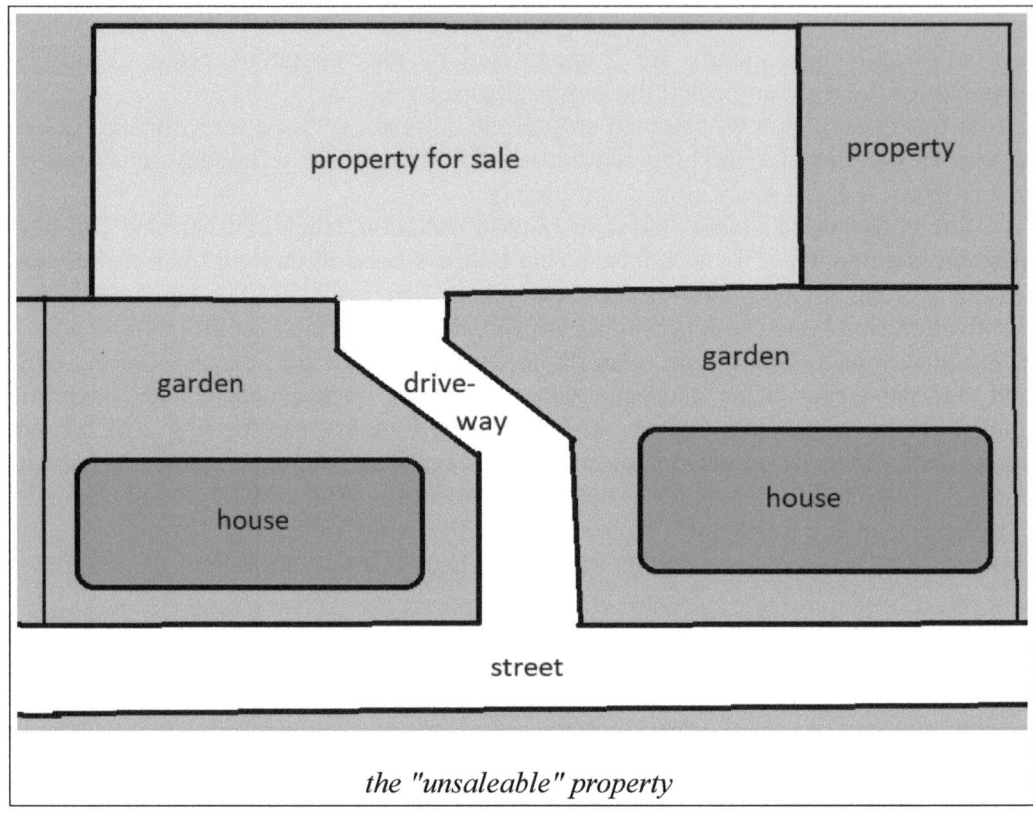

the "unsaleable" property

After I had delimited the property from the neighbors with the help of the Lesser Pentagram Ritual and then, with the help of imagination and incense, had enlivened the property and, above all, connected it with the street, the property was sold a few weeks later.

After the Feng Shui treatment the property was no longer secluded, inaccessible and foreign-occupied, but a quiet and well protected place to live – an almost ideal building plot …

II 11. d)   The intensity of the place-effect

This point is the most difficult to assess. Every place has an effect as the previous three points show. However, the person who lives in this place still has his self-determination as well. If the place has a great effect, it is more difficult to do what one wants in it anyway. If one has a strong will, it is easier to assert oneself.

Basically, the pragmatic approach makes the most sense here:

- If you move into a new apartment, share a new studio, set up a new work-shop, etc., it makes sense and saves effort later on to check the quality of the place once and possibly give it a new imprint.

- If something in a place simply does not want to work at all or only with great effort, one should also consider that there is something wrong with the place.

- If one wants to achieve a very high performance in a place (stock market speculation, healing room, temple, etc.), it makes sense to also imprint the room in such a way that it forms an optimal basis.

- If one wants to achieve a very high performance in a place, it makes sense to also look for the best possible place – and afterwards imprint it as well as possible.

Finally, it makes sense to know and consider the influence of a place and neither to ignore nor to overestimate this influence and not to let oneself go crazy because of a missing area in the upper right corner and to believe that one cannot achieve anything in this place.

In order to be able to correctly assess the influence of a location, there is really only one way to go: experimentation, practice and experience – which ultimately leads to a solid sense of craftsmanship.

III   Designing

The diagnosis is now followed by the therapy: If you have recognized the quality of a place and want to change it, you need several things.

III 1.   The place

In the beginning, of course, there is the place itself and either one's own motivation or the order from its owner to change this place.

This is usually followed by visiting the place and observing and describing its quality using the methods presented in Part II of this book.

III 2.   The goal

The second step sounds very simple, but it is usually not that easy to grasp: How should the place become?

III 2. a)   The search for the goal

In order to be able to change a place in the right way, a clear goal is needed, i.e. a description of the optimal state of the place that is as profound as possible. The clarification of this question alone usually takes a whole hour. The following points are clues for this "clarifying conversation" between the Feng Shui expert and the owner of the place in question:

- What do you want to do in this place?
- What quality do you want to achieve with this activity?
- How do you want to feel with this quality?
- Do you already know this quality and if so, from where?
- Do you have a picture for this quality?
- What "conducive environment" should be part of this quality?

It is important not to take the owner's first answer to the question about his goal as the ultimately valid answer, because usually people do not answer with their actual goal, but only with the path they want to take towards this goal:

- If someone wants a high fence, he probably wants security. If he wants security, he may feel weak himself. If he feels himself weak, he may repress his aggression, etc.

- If someone wants to earn more money with his job, one can ask what he wants to use the money for, how much he actually works, how effective his work is – and what his ideal for a good life would be. In doing so, you should ask the person several times to really wish without any inhibitions – without any consideration of whether his wishes might be realizable or not.

- If someone wants a splendid house with an equally splendid garden, he may simply be seeking recognition. This in turn suggests self-doubt. These self-doubts will in turn have a deeper cause, and so on.

- If someone wants to have a protection against "evil spirits", then he is obviously afraid of something. This "something" must be found out more precisely in order to be able to do anything effective. Apparently the person also feels threatened and helpless – why?

Here the consultant is required to have psychological knowledge and skills, otherwise it is not possible to create what the owner really needs. It is about the person recognizing and expressing what he really wants, what he desires from the bottom of his heart – only these goals are really sustainable and worth the effort necessary to achieve them.

Such clear orders as "I want to sell this property." or "I want this place to stop being haunted." are rather rare.

III 2. b)   The search for the image

Once the actual goal has been found and formulated in as distinctive a way as possible, the next step is to concretize the goal into an image that expresses the goal in a direct, vivid and convincing way.

This step may also take a long time, because only a few people are familiar with creating such images.

This process of "image design" is probably best explained by two examples:

example 1

- An entrepreneur, who is groaning under the burden of his work, comes to the conclusion after a long conversation that he constantly has the feeling of wandering around in a fog and not knowing what to do next, how to cope with the mountains of forms of the city administration etc., how to keep track of his employees, and so on.

Finally, it turns out that his ideal image is the commander's hill, from which the commander sees and directs his army and can also clearly see the entire relevant surroundings.

- Then we looked for what image he has of himself – it was the image of a druid. His desk in the picture was a big stone slab, on which were all the things he needed for his activity.

- Behind him was protective forest, but there were gaps through which he could look into the distance. To the front, as well as to the left and to the right, he had a clear view.

- Then we looked at the place itself and added a fireplace and a spring. There was also a resting place for his power animal. Finally, paths and trails were added that led into the distance and by which he was connected to everyone and everything.

example 2

- A friend of mine, after a long contemplation, realized that she needed a nest in a tall tree as her home – she has a large bird of prey as her power animal …

- Then we looked for the type of tree in which this nest is located.

- In this nest there were some places with different qualities, partition walls, shelters, etc., all designed as parts of the nest.

Other possible "inner images" for places are, for example, the half-timbered house, the castle, the badger's lair, the pirate ship, the spaceship, the caravan, the witch's cottage, the forest house, the wizard's tower – there are no limits to the imagination …

To find the right image, it is necessary to make it clear to the person seeking advice that he should wish as uninhibitedly as possible – only then will his wish come close to what his heart actually wants.

One can also consult the horoscope of the person concerned – in this case the element of the ascendant and the planets in the 2nd house are of particular importance for the design of the "inner ideal picture", since the ascendant indicates the element from which the ideal place is built, and the planets in the 2nd house show which forces ideally work at that place.

The following are just a few examples of the possible preferences of the Ascendants and the planets in the 2nd house:

Ascendants:
- *Fire* (Aries, Leo, Sagittarius): fireplace, hearth, volcano, firewalking place, steam engine, etc.
- *Water* (Cancer, Scorpio, Pisces): sea, island, lake, pond, river, island, ship, etc.
- *Air* (Libra, Aquarius, Gemini): coast, mountain top, tree top, nest, airplane, etc.
- *Earth* (Capricorn, Taurus, Virgo): field, mountain, valley, cave, building, garden, park, etc.

Planets in 2nd house:
- *Moon*: waters, security, nest, cave
- *Mercury*: meeting place, school, library
- *Venus*: beautiful house, rose garden, flowers
- *Sun*: palace, center, capital
- *Mars*: tournament place, sports field, horses, tents
- *Jupiter*: office, commander's hill, observation tower
- *Saturn*: castle, city with walls, rocks
- *Uranus*: spaceship, submarine, distant planet
- *Neptune*: ship, temple, church, artist's studio
- *Pluto*: volcano, control center, a place before God's throne

These are, of course, only a few suggestions, which can in no way replace one's own experience with the interpretation of horoscopes.

III 3.   The purification of the place

If one wants to change a place, one will usually begin by dissolving what one wants to change, i.e., by purifying the place of what is undesirable.

III 3. a)   The physical purification

Often there are simple measures that already help significantly, such as cleaning a place, re-wallpapering an apartment, taking away garbage that was on the property, and the like.

It becomes a little more differentiated, if one takes out certain furniture, on which memories of unpleasant events are clinging, if one cleans up one's files, lets one's PC be repaired, cuts out the dead wood in the trees in the garden, weeds, cleans out the cellar, cancels superfluous insurance contracts, sorts out long expired spices and supplies and so on.

These more or less simple physical actions can already change the mood of a place.

III 3. b)   The purification of the life force

With the purification of the life force in a place, the "magic part" of Feng Shui begins.

First, one looks at what one can perceive in a place – for this, the dream journey is an important tool. If there are particular individual obstacles such as a spirit of a dead person haunting the house, or the influence of a nearby garbage dump or sewage treatment plant, then one should start with these points.

In the cases mentioned, this would be, for example, escorting the deceased to the afterlife – if he had been a Christian, one can bring him inwardly to Christ, if his religion had been Islam, one could ask Mohammed to receive him, etc.

If there is a nearby garbage dump or sewage treatment plant, one can build a "dam" of life force between the house and the garbage dump or sewage treatment plant and divert the radiation from these unpleasant places. In doing so, one must see what is possible and how this can best be accomplished, i.e. which imagination works best.

Sometimes it is also necessary to first look more closely at the relationship between the undesirable influence from outside and the one to whom the place to be cleansed belongs. This would be the case, for example, if someone lives in the neighborhood of a concentration camp, next to a slaughterhouse or on a battlefield from the Second World War, or in a house that was built in a place where a prison or a psychiatric ward had previously stood. In such extreme cases, there may be something in the owner of the place that attracted him to that special place. Without becoming aware of this connection and resolving it, all Feng Shui measures may have very limited effect.

One should also pay attention to what has created the life force imprint in a place. For example, if it is a permanent dispute between tenant and landlord, it might be necessary to take care of this issue as well in order to change the quality in that place.

Sometimes it is also the biography of the owner or proprietor on the place, which causes the imprint of the place and the stories at it – sometimes the consideration of the horoscope of this owner or proprietor helps or a longer conversation with him, but such backgrounds often lead then to completely different problems, topics and tasks than only to Feng Shui.

One can also use traditional methods for the general life force cleansing of a place, such as the Lesser Pentagram Ritual, the somewhat gentler Rose-Cross Ritual, the very old Indian Agnihotra Ritual, the also very old ritual of the four Egyptian protective goddesses Isis, Nephthys, Neith and Selket, the Christian cleansing with holy water and incense, etc., which is common in this country. One should preferably use the ritual that one is already familiar with.

If the imprinting of a place resembles a huge garbage dump (e.g., if one is to cleanse a whole farm), one can also use undifferentiated but powerful measures: imaginatively burn the imprinted life force at the place, let it blow away by an imagined storm, let it be washed away by an imagined flood, or let it be absorbed by the earth. The more intensively one calls the used element and the more differentiated and at the more individual places one imagines the effect of this element, the stronger will be the effect of this purification.

If there are individual stubborn life-force forms in a place that cannot be dissolved, one can imgainatively place them in an imagined silver bowl in a neutral place and then blast this life-force form in it. In very stubborn cases, one can also imagine an atomic bomb explosion to dissolve the life force imprint in one place. However, one should first try it in the gentler ways …

III 4. The change of the physical situation

When the place has been cleansed physically and has been also cleansed in respect to the life force, the actual transformation begins.

If there are simple ways to change something physically such as by rearranging some furniture or filling a hole in the property with soil, then that should be done first. However, some physical changes are a bit more troublesome – in which case they should be done when it can be arranged.

There are many possibilities when physically changing a place:

- One can plant a dense hedge to demarcate it from an adjacent place with an unpleasant aura.

- One can disperse the hard life force, which has been created e.g. by a long straight road or the like, and which points exactly to a plot of land, by a dozen differently directed small mirrors. You can also plant a big tree in front of this place at the edge of the plot or put a big rock there. If the plot is very large, you could also plant a small pond there to absorb the hard life force.

- One can place in a niche in the house wall or in the hallway again a holy figure, a statue of a god or the like, in order to fill up this emphasized and therefore influential place again with a desired quality, which then radiates from there.

- You can invite the four elements to a place in different ways if you want them to be there:

- *Fire*: fire pit, hearth, fireplace, candle, Agni statue, incense-work, ace of wands (Tarot card), fire poster, etc.

- *Water*: indoor fountain, pond, fountain, ace of cups (Tarot card), water poster, etc.

- *Air*: essential oil fragrance lamp, sound chimes, aeolian harp, ace of swords (Tarot card), wind poster, etc.

- *Earth*: crystals, flower pots, stones, coin, ace of coins (Tarot card), earth poster, etc.

- One can set up a place for one's power animal, power plant and power stone.

- One can set up a house altar – it usually belongs where the TV or the wide screen monitor is nowadays …

In general, one can consult the analytical study of the place and see where support, mitigation, supplementation, etc. of the already existing qualities is needed.

Sometimes, however, one finds things that cannot be changed, such as high-voltage pylons with power lines running nearby. Here you can experiment to see what measures have an effect – e.g. put a wire all around the property to divert the voltages. But as I said – in some situations that one finds, one can only try out and see what has an effect …

III 5.   The change of the vital force

The change of the life force is based on at least six things, but other aspects can be added if needed:

1. a clear intention,
2. a suitable image for this intention,
3. the imagination of this image,
4. a single-minded will focused on this image,
5. possibly the invocation of a deity to help with this, and
6. possibly physical aids that support the imagination.

III 5. a)   Imprinting the place with the image

Imprinting a place with the chosen ideal image is a magical process that is ultimately the same as charging a talisman or consecrating an amulet – or consecrating a church or temple.

If you have a contact with a deity through meditations, rituals, dream journeys, dreams and the like, you can ask them to help you with the consecration.

Then you should see if you can find a gesture that can symbolize the life force imprint and that fits well to you. This can be, for example, touching with a crystal (earth element), breathing on the place to be imprinted or fanning with a feather (air element), sprinkling with water (water element) or lighting a match (fire element).

One can also have this gesture consecrated by a deity. Thus, I find it extremely effective to draw a circle with a lit match with a cross in it in the air in front of me ($\oplus$), asking Shiva to consecrate this fire. After that, I then imprint each place in the place with the help of such a lighted match, with which I draw this symbol in the air during my imagination of the desired image. These matches are, so to speak, one-way magic wands.

This imprinting of the place with the help of mostly only one method, which one feels most comfortable with, is the foundation of most Feng Shui treatments of the life force at a place.

For example, if you imagine an apartment as an eagle's eyrie at the top of a tree, you can imagine a branch of this tree at each corner of the room, at each doorpost and at the side of each window, lighting a matchstick there (or using another imagination gesture).

In this way, step by step, all the elements of the selected ideal image are imagined in their places. One should take one's time and proceed thoroughly, so that the imagined picture gradually becomes really alive inside.

There is one help that is essential in the whole process: one should always understand the imagination as an expression of what the soul of the owner or possessor of the place wants in this life. In this way the imagination gets a root in the soul of the person concerned, which has the effect that this imagination does not simply dissolve after a few days. The connection of the imagination to the soul of the client is the root that gives support to the imagination and lets it grow. This alignment also has the advantage that one is not so inclined to use one's own life force for the imagination.

The source of the life force is the deity one has asked for help; the soul of the client is the owner of the Feng Shui image; the magician or witch who performs the Feng Shui is the architect and the builder of the imagination.

III 5. b)   The four elements

One can also invoke the four elements instead of a deity or complementary to it and ask for help. This is best done in the tradition with which one is most familiar. For example, if this were to be the Lesser Pentagram Ritual, it would be the four Archangels Michael (Fire), Gabriel (Water), Raphael (Air) and Auriel (Earth).

III 5. c)   Spirits of animals, plants and minerals

Situations often arise in which one feels that a certain quality is needed. In these cases it is useful to see where one can find this quality.

Such a case is, for example, the calming of the mood in a place, that is, the need to harmonize a place. In these cases, dabbing a little rose massage oil from Weleda on the place in question has proven to be effective. The feeling of harmony then comes almost by itself ...

Possibly clarity is also needed in one place. Then one could call the quality of a rock crystal to this place – whereby it will probably be a help to hold a rock crystal in the hand. (For the qualities of the different minerals see the books of Michael Gienger).

If someone often receives visitors at their desk or takes phone calls and lacks authority, you can imagine a life-size tiger to the left and right of the desk each – this works wonders.

Also with these imaginations one should look that one anchors the imagined picture in some way in the intentions of the client, so that the picture becomes stable.

III 5. d)   Personal spirit beings

The easiest way to anchor an imagination is, of course, using the mineral that is the power stone of the client, the plant that is the power plant of the client, and the animal that is the power animal of the client.

But of course you have to see if the power stone fits to the desired structure you want to establish, if the power plant fits to the desired attitude, and if the power animal to the desired dynamics – which will, of course, fit in most cases.

For more personal places that are to be imprinted with the help of Feng Shui, one can see if there are three suitable places for these three spirit allies of the owner in the place. This is not always the case, but if it fits well, it will greatly increase the radiance of the place in question.

III 5. e)   The soul

In most cases there will be no special place for the soul, since the soul is in the person concerned and has already played the formative role in the design of the image to be imagined.

As a rule, there will be a special place for the soul only when a house altar or the like is erected.

III 5. f)   External contacts

One can also include things and places that are close to the place to be imprinted. For example, there may be a stream, a pond with water lilies, a large oak tree, etc., near a house that has a special appearance and whose quality you want to include in the imprint.

In this case, one should not simply "tap" the life force of, for example, this tree, but turn to the oak elf in this tree in a short dream journey and talk to him about it. If this elf agrees to imprint a part of the house with his quality, then this imprinting will also be much more stable than it would be by simply "tapping the life force" of this tree.

III 5. g)   Homeopathic remedies

Sometimes there are quite specific problems such as a huge oil tank in the basement whose radiation fills the entire house.

Oil, natural gas and coal have been formed from plants that grew on the earth a long time ago. Most of these plants have been lycopods.

Therefore, in such a case, you can turn to the lycopod elf and ask him for help – which is, of course, easiest if you already know him through dream journeys and the like.

To achieve the dissolution of the imprinting of the house by the huge oil tank, one can also obtain the homeopathic remedy "Lycopodium C200", which has been prepared from Lycopodium. This remedy can then be dissolved in water and sprayed while asking the Lycopodium elf in the basement room with the oil tank.

If there are such special problems, one can generally see if there is a suitable homeopathic remedy. One can use these remedies both for purification and for imprinting – one invites in both cases the quality of the substance from which the remedy has been made.

In most cases, the potency "C200" will be well suited, as it roughly corresponds to the soul of the substance, i.e. the mother goddess of the animal species, the elf of the plant species or the "dwarf" of the mineral species.

If you can't think of any suitable gestures or any other suitable procedure, you can simply dissolve the homeopathic remedy in a glass of water and then spray this water in the place in question. This effect is strengthened if one sings alone or with others the sounds that come to one or if you just vibrate an „a".

III 5. h)   Deities

A special role can be played by the patron deity of the client, that is, the deity from whose "sea" the soul of the client is a "drop". However, this is usually the case only with house altars and temples – and if this patron deity is known to the client.

Statues of deities, spirits, saints, etc. that play a major role in the religion of the person concerned can be an important help in imprinting a place. Of course, one should not just put a Buddha statue in a corner and leave it at that, but choose a suitable place for it and then also consecrate this statue, i.e. call Buddha into this statue – either with a ritual or with a dream journey.

Possibly one can also connect certain elements of the place to be imprinted with mythological elements. For example, on a Texas ranch whose owner feels closely connected to the Germanic religion, there is a large tree which she has equated with the world ash tree Yggdrasil and which she also calls "Yggdrasil".

Such identifications can be an effective tool in imprinting a place. For example, all elements of the ancient Egyptian temples have been equated to a part of the world and often also to an element from mythology. This makes the temple a sacred place, rich in life force.

III 5. i)   Symbols

One can also use symbols and simple shapes to imprint a place. Ancient symbols such as the planetary signs, the signs of the zodiac, the Egyptian hieroglyphs, the hexagrams of the I Ching, etc., but also, for example, the crop circle symbolism are suitable for this. One can also, like Marco Pogacnik, design one's own "geomantic sign language" and then engrave it on stones and place them in the places to be imprinted.

III 5. j)   Earth Kundalini

When you have finished imagining the picture in a place and it feels round, you can still finally a connection to the earth center. The glowing iron/nickel core of the earth is the root chakra of the earth. When one sends a ray of light down into this earth core from the imprinted place, one makes contact with the root chakra of the earth. From there, one can then call up the life force that belongs to that place and that wants to express itself in that place.

In most cases, this ascending force can be seen as a dragon – more rarely as a snake or as fire or lava. These dragons are the same motif of life force flow as in the Chinese "riding of the dragon" that has already been described.

By this Feng Shui version of Kundalini Yoga, a place becomes very charged and once again changes its quality – just like a bud unfolding into a flower.

This calling of the earth kundalini should always be done at the very end, when the imagined picture is finished, when all ambiguities have been discussed with the client, and when all wishes that the client has become aware of during the imprinting have been carried out.

III 5. k)   Creativity

The examples given in this book clearly show that in Feng Shui, as in all areas of life, it is important to find one's own style and to become creative. However, this can hardly be achieved without a lot of experimentation and plenty of personal experience.

There are many methods, symbols, best practices, etc. in Feng Shui, but the most important element is your own experience. If you want to learn Feng Shui, you should just start using it and see what effect it has. You may find that "astrological Feng Shui" suits you best, or that the Tarot cards are the most helpful, or you may learn to perceive the life force flowing in the earth through the crop circles, or it may be the traditional Chinese method that suits you best... or you may gradually develop a completely new approach.

It is not a certain system, not a certain deity, not a certain doctrine by which one can learn Feng Shui.

It is one's own experience that can make one's Feng Shui safe, solid and effective.

English Books by Harry Eilenstein

- Living Magic (261 p.)	- Mandalas for Beginners (76 p.)
- The Synthesis of Physics and Magic (192 p.)	- Crop Circles for Beginners (344 p.)
- Telepathy for Beginners (60 p.)	- Feng Shui for Beginners (96 p.)
- Telepathy for Advanced Learners (52 p.)	
- Telekinesis for Beginners (56 p.)	**These books will be puplished soon:**
- Astral Projection for Beginners (60 p.)	- Life Force for Beginners
- Meditation for Beginners (60 p.)	- Kundalini for Beginners
- Prophecy for Beginners (60 p.)	- Chakra-Magic for Beginners
- Invocations for Beginners (52 p.)	- Astrology for Beginners
- Evocations for Beginners (62 p.)	- Ritual Magic for Beginners
- Auto-Movement for Beginners (60 p.)	- Magic Research for Beginners
- Elves for Beginners (56 p.)	- Symbolism of Numbers for Beginners
- Hypnosis for Beginners (56 p.)	- Language of the Moon – for Beginners
- Love Magic for Beginners (52 p.)	- Magic Chant for Beginners
- Money Magic for Beginners (60 p.)	- Da'ath-Magic for Beginners
- Magic Objects for Beginners (64 p.)	- Magic for Beginners – Anthology I
- Shamanism for Beginners (52 p.)	- Magic for Beginners – Anthology II
- Self Knowledge for Beginners (60 p.)	- Magic for Beginners – Anthology III
- Number Symbolism for Beginners (64 p.)	- Magic for Beginners – Anthology IV

Bücher von Harry Eilenstein

Religion allgemein
- Die sieben Schritte des Lebens (428 S.)
- Muttergöttin und Schamanen (168 S.)
- Göbekli Tepe (472 S.)
- Die Göttin von Göbekli Tepe (144 S.)
- Totempfähle (440 S.)
- Christus (60 S.)
- Dakini (80 S.)
- Vajra (76 S.)

Ägypten
- Hathor und Re 1: Götter und Mythen im Alten Ägypten (432 S.)
- Hathor und Re 2: Die altägyptische Religion – Ursprünge, Kult und Magie (396 S.)
- Isis (508 S.)

Indogermanen
- Die Entwicklung der indogermanischen Religionen (700 S.)
- Wurzeln und Zweige der indogermanischen Religion (224 S.)

Germanen
- Die Götter der Germanen (87 Bände – siehe nächste Seite)
- Odin (300 S.)

Kelten
- Cernunnos (690 S.)
- Taliesin (228 S.)
- Der Kessel von Gundestrup (220 S.)
- Der Chiemsee-Kessel (76)

Psychologie
- Über die Freude (100 S.)
- Das Geheimnis des inneren Friedens (252 S.)
- Das Beziehungsmandala (52 S.)
- Gefühle und ihre Verwandlungen (404 S.)
- einsgerichtet (140 S.)
- Liebe und Eigenständigkeit (216 S.)
- Von innerer Fülle zu äußerem Gedeihen (52 S.)

Heilung
- Die Symbolik der Krankheiten (76 S.)

Kunst
- Herz des Tanzes – Tanz des Herzens (160 S.)

Drama
- König Athelstan (104 S.)

Bücher von Harry Eilenstein

„Magie für Anfänger"	Magie
- Telepathie für Anfänger (60 S.)	- Handbuch für Zauberlehrlinge (408 S.)
- Telepathie für Fortgeschrittene (52 S.)	- Tarot (104 S.)
- Telekinese für Anfänger (52 S.)	- Physik und Magie (184 S.)
- Lebenskraft für Anfänger (60 S.)	- Die Synthese von Physik und Magie (200S.)
- Meditation für Anfänger (56 S.)	- Die Magie-Formel (156 S.)
- Kundalini für Anfänger (100 S.)	- Krafttiere – Tiergöttinnen – Tiertänze (112 S.)
- Hypnose für Anfänger (56 S.)	- Schwitzhütten (524 S.)
- Auto-Movement für Anfänger (56 S.)	- Mythen und Magie der Harfe (116 S.)
- Chakra-Magie für Anfänger (148 S.)	- Magie heute – Berichte aus der Praxis (288 S.)
- Astralreisen für Anfänger (56 S.)	**Meditation**
- Astrologie für Anfänger (120 S.)	- Der Lebenskraftkörper (230 S.)
- Ritual-Magie für Anfänger (56 S.)	- Die Chakren (100 S.)
- Mandalas für Anfänger (68 S.)	- Das Chakren-System mit den Nebenchakren
- Geldzauber für Anfänger (56 S.)	(296 S.)
- Liebeszauber für Anfänger (52 S.)	- Organe und Chakren (64 S.)
- Invokationen für Anfänger (52 S.)	- Die platonischen Körper in den Chakren (156 S.)
- Evokationen für Anfänger (60 S.)	- Meditation (140 S.)
- Elfen für Anfänger (56 S.)	- Drachenfeuer (124 S.)
- Magie-Forschung für Anfänger (140 S.)	- Kundalini I (676 S.)
- Selbsterkenntnis für Anfänger (52 S.)	- Reinkarnation (156 S.)
- Zahlensymbolik für Anfänger (60 S.)	- einsgerichtet (140 S.)
- Die Sprache des Mondes – für Anfänger (116 S.)	**Astrologie**
- Zaubergesänge für Anfänger (100 S.)	- Astrologie (496 S.)
- Zukunftschau für Anfänger (60 S.)	- Photo-Astrologie (428 S.)
- Schamanismus für Anfänger (52 S.)	- Die astrologischen Aspekte (88 S.)
- Magische Gegenstände für Anfänger (68 S.)	- Horoskop und Seele (120 S.)
- Da'ath-Magie für Anfänger (64 S.)	**Kabbala**
- Kornkreise für Anfänger (348 S.)	- Kursus der praktischen Kabbala (150 S.)
- Feng Shui für Anfänger (96 S.)	- Eltern der Erde (450 S.)
- Magie für Anfänger – Sammelband I (696 S.)	- Blüten des Lebensbaumes:
- Magie für Anfänger – Sammelband II (664 S.)	- Die Struktur des kabbalistischen
- Magie für Anfänger – Sammelband III (580 S.)	Lebensbaumes (370 S.)
„Traumreisen"	- Der kabbalistische Lebensbaum als
- Traumreisen zu Heilpflanzen (700 S.)	Forschungshilfsmittel (580 S.)
	- Der kabbalistische Lebensbaum als
	spirituelle Landkarte (520 S.)

Die Themen der 87 Bände der Reihe „Die Götter der Germanen"